ASP.NET Web API Security Essentials

Take the security of your ASP.NET Web API to the next level using some of the most amazing security techniques around

Rajesh Gunasundaram

[PACKT] open source*
PUBLISHING   community experience distilled

BIRMINGHAM - MUMBAI

ASP.NET Web API Security Essentials

First published: November 2015

Production reference: 1241115

Published by Packt Publishing Ltd.
Livery Place
35 Livery Street
Birmingham B3 2PB, UK.

ISBN 978-1-78588-221-0

www.packtpub.com

Credits

Author
Rajesh Gunasundaram

Reviewer
Anuraj Parameswaran

Commissioning Editor
Amarabha Banerjee

Acquisition Editor
Prachi Bisht

Content Development Editor
Anish Dhurat

Technical Editor
Danish Shaikh

Copy Editor
Vibha Shukla

Project Coordinator
Harshal Ved

Proofreader
Safis Editing

Indexer
Mariammal Chettiyar

Production Coordinator
Nilesh Mohite

Cover Work
Nilesh Mohite

About the Author

Rajesh Gunasundaram is a software architect, technical writer and blogger. He has over 13 years of experience in the IT industry, with more than 10 years using Microsoft's .NET and 2 years of using BizTalk Server, and a year of iOS application development.

Rajesh is a founder and an editor of technical blogs: www.programmerguide.net and www.ioscorner.com. You can find many of his technical writings on .NET and iOS.

Rajesh holds a master's degree in computer application and began his career as a software engineer in the year 2002. He has worked on client premises located in various countries, such as the UK, Belarus, and Norway. He is also experienced in developing mobile applications for iPhone and iPad.

His technical strengths include Objective-C, C#, ASP.NET MVC, Web API, WCF, .Net Framework 4.5, AngularJS, BizTalk, SQL Server, REST, SOA, design patterns, and software architecture.

Acknowledgments

I am greatly thankful to my beloved and wonderful friend Ahila Dhayalan, who has constantly encouraged and motivated me while writing this book. She put me back on track whenever I deviated from my schedule of submitting the chapters. Without her support and encouragement, this book wouldn't have been possible.

I am also thankful to the entire team at Packt Publishing for providing me the opportunity to author this book.

Thanks to Prachi Bisht for having confidence in me and giving me the opportunity to write this book.

Thanks to Ajinkya Paranjape for having high regard for me and providing invaluable assistance.

Thanks to Anish Dhurat for guiding and helping me to shape the content of the book.

Thanks to Danish Shaikh for verifying the technical content and bringing it to a good shape.

About the Reviewer

Anuraj Parameswaran works as an architect in Orion India Systems Pvt. Ltd., Kochi. He has extensive experience of more than ten years in working on different technologies, mostly in the Microsoft space. He has been working on the .NET platform since its early days. He leads the technology and innovation team at Orion. He is a cofounder of MobiThoughts, a mobile application development company. His focus areas are data analytics, architecture, and Cloud computing.

He writes about technology in his popular blog at http://www.dotnetthoughts. net/. He is a *K-MUG Community Council* member and an active volunteer in *Microsoft Technology Community*.

www.PacktPub.com

Support files, eBooks, discount offers, and more

For support files and downloads related to your book, please visit www.PacktPub.com.

Did you know that Packt offers eBook versions of every book published, with PDF and ePub files available? You can upgrade to the eBook version at www.PacktPub.com and as a print book customer, you are entitled to a discount on the eBook copy. Get in touch with us at service@packtpub.com for more details.

At www.PacktPub.com, you can also read a collection of free technical articles, sign up for a range of free newsletters and receive exclusive discounts and offers on Packt books and eBooks.

https://www2.packtpub.com/books/subscription/packtlib

Do you need instant solutions to your IT questions? PacktLib is Packt's online digital book library. Here, you can search, access, and read Packt's entire library of books.

Why subscribe?

- Fully searchable across every book published by Packt
- Copy and paste, print, and bookmark content
- On demand and accessible via a web browser

Free access for Packt account holders

If you have an account with Packt at www.PacktPub.com, you can use this to access PacktLib today and view 9 entirely free books. Simply use your login credentials for immediate access.

*I would like to dedicate this book to my wife, Sairabanu, and my brothers,
Magesh and Nithish, as they are my driving factors.*

Table of Contents

Preface

ASP.NET Web API is a framework that makes it easy to build HTTP services that reach a broad range of clients, including browsers and mobile devices. It is an ideal platform to build RESTful applications on the .NET Framework.

This book provides a practical guide to secure your ASP.NET Web API by various security techniques, such as integrating the ASP.NET Identity system, implementing various authentication mechanisms, enabling **Secured Socket Layer** (**SSL**), preventing cross-site request forgery attacks, and enabling cross-origin resource sharing.

What this book covers

Chapter 1, *Setting up a Browser Client*, helps you to set up a browser client in order to use Web API services. It also covers ASP.NET Web API Security Architecture and authentication, and authorization to secure a web API from unauthorized users.

Chapter 2, *Enabling SSL for ASP.NET Web API*, explains how to use SSL with ASP. NET Web API, including using SSL client certificates. There are several common authentication schemes that are not secured over plain HTTP in particular Basic authentication and forms authentication, which send unencrypted credentials. In order to be secure, these authentication schemes must use SSL. In addition to this, SSL client certificates can be used to authenticate clients.

Chapter 3, *Integrating ASP.NET Identity System with ASP.NET Web API*, explains how to integrate the ASP.NET Identity system with ASP.NET Web API. The ASP. NET Identity system is designed to replace the previous ASP.NET Membership and Simple Membership systems. It includes profile support and OAuth integration. It works with OWIN and is included with ASP.NET templates that are shipped with Visual Studio 2013 and later versions.

Chapter 4, Securing a web API using OAuth2, shows you how to secure a web API using OAuth2 to authenticate against a membership database using the OWIN middleware. You will be able to use local logins to send authenticated requests using OAuth2.

Chapter 5, Enabling Basic Authentication using Authentication Filters in Web API, covers how to set an authentication scheme for individual controllers or actions using Authentication filters. This chapter shows an authentication filter that implements the HTTP Basic Access Authentication scheme. It will also cover the advantages and disadvantages of using Basic Authentication.

Chapter 6, Securing a Web API using Forms and Windows Authentication, explains how to secure a web API using Forms Authentication and how users can log in with their Windows credentials using Integrated Windows Authentication. You will also get to learn the advantages and disadvantages of using Forms and Windows Authentication in Web API. Forms authentication uses an HTML form to send the user's credentials to the server. Integrated Windows Authentication enables the users to log in with their Windows credentials, using Kerberos or NTLM. The client sends credentials in the Authorization header. Windows authentication is best suited for an intranet environment.

Chapter 7, Using External Authentication Services with ASP.NET Web API, helps you to understand the need for external authentication services in order to enable OAuth/ OpenID and social media authentication. Using external authentication services helps in reducing development time when creating new web applications. Web users typically have several existing accounts for popular web services and social media websites; therefore, when a web application implements the authentication services from an external web service or social media website, it saves the development time that would have been spent while creating an authentication implementation. Using an external authentication service saves the end users from creating another account for the web application and having to remember yet another username and password.

Chapter 8, Preventing Cross-Site Request Forgery (CSRF) Attacks in Web API, helps you to implement anti-CSRF measures in ASP.NET Web API. Using an API key-based authentication, or a more sophisticated mechanism such as OAuth, helps in preventing CSRF attacks. ASP.NET MVC uses anti-forgery tokens, which are also called request verification tokens.

Chapter 9, Enabling Cross-Origin Resource Sharing (CORS) in ASP.NET Web API, explains how to enable CORS in your Web API application. Browser security prevents a web page from making AJAX requests to another domain. This restriction is called the same-origin policy and prevents a malicious site from reading sensitive data from another site. However, sometimes you might want to let other sites call your web API.

What you need for this book

Software requirements for development:

- Visual Studio 2013 or Later version
- Windows 7 or Later version

Hardware requirements for development:

- 1.6 GHz or faster processor
- 1 GB of RAM (1.5 GB if running on a virtual machine)
- 10 GB (NTFS) of the available hard disk space
- 5400 RPM hard drive
- DirectX 9-capable video card running at 1024 x 768 or higher display resolution

Who this book is for

This book is intended for everyone having the knowledge of developing an ASP.NET Web API application. Good working knowledge and experience with C# and the .NET framework are prerequisites in order to learn from this book.

Conventions

In this book, you will find a number of text styles that distinguish between different kinds of information. Here are some examples of these styles and explanations of their meanings.

Code words in text, database table names, folder names, filenames, file extensions, pathnames, dummy URLs, user input, and Twitter handles are shown as follows: "We can include other contexts through the use of the `include` directive."

A block of code is set as follows:

```
[default]
exten => s,1,Dial(Zap/1|30)
exten => s,2,Voicemail(u100)
exten => s,102,Voicemail(b100)
exten => i,1,Voicemail(s0)
```

When we wish to draw your attention to a particular part of a code block, the relevant lines or items are set in bold:

```
[default]
exten => s,1,Dial(Zap/1|30)
exten => s,2,Voicemail(u100)
exten => s,102,Voicemail(b100)
exten => i,1,Voicemail(s0)
```

Any command-line input or output is written as follows:

```
# cp /usr/src/asterisk-addons/configs/cdr_mysql.conf.sample
    /etc/asterisk/cdr_mysql.conf
```

New terms and **important words** are shown in bold. Words that you see on the screen, for example, in menus or dialog boxes, appear in the text like this: "Clicking the **Next** button moves you to the next screen."

> Warnings or important notes appear in a box like this.

> Tips and tricks appear like this.

Reader feedback

Feedback from our readers is always welcome. Let us know what you think about this book—what you liked or disliked. Reader feedback is important for us as it helps us develop titles that you will really get the most out of.

To send us general feedback, simply e-mail feedback@packtpub.com and mention the book's title in the subject of your message.

If there is a topic that you have expertise in and you are interested in either writing or contributing to a book, see our author guide at www.packtpub.com/authors.

Customer support

Now that you are the proud owner of a Packt book, we have a number of things to help you to get the most from your purchase.

Downloading the example code

You can download the example code files from your account at `http://www.packtpub.com` for all the Packt Publishing books you have purchased. If you purchased this book elsewhere, you can visit `http://www.packtpub.com/support` and register to have the files e-mailed directly to you.

Downloading the color images of this book

We also provide you with a PDF file that has color images of the screenshots/diagrams used in this book. The color images will help you better understand the changes in the output. You can download this file from `http://www.packtpub.com/sites/default/files/downloads/12340T_ColorImages.pdf`.

Errata

Although we have taken every care to ensure the accuracy of our content, mistakes do happen. If you find a mistake in one of our books—maybe a mistake in the text or the code—we would be grateful if you could report this to us. By doing so, you can save other readers from frustration and help us improve subsequent versions of this book. If you find any errata, please report them by visiting `http://www.packtpub.com/submit-errata`, selecting your book, clicking on the **Errata Submission Form** link, and entering the details of your errata. Once your errata are verified, your submission will be accepted and the errata will be uploaded to our website or added to any list of existing errata under the Errata section of that title.

To view the previously submitted errata, go to `https://www.packtpub.com/books/content/support` and enter the name of the book in the search field. The required information will appear under the **Errata** section.

Piracy

Piracy of copyrighted material on the Internet is an ongoing problem across all media. At Packt, we take the protection of our copyright and licenses very seriously. If you come across any illegal copies of our works in any form on the Internet, please provide us with the location address or website name immediately so that we can pursue a remedy.

Please contact us at copyright@packtpub.com with a link to the suspected pirated material.

We appreciate your help in protecting our authors and our ability to bring you valuable content.

Questions

If you have a problem with any aspect of this book, you can contact us at questions@packtpub.com, and we will do our best to address the problem.

1
Setting up a Browser Client

If you are reading this book, it is because you understand the importance of securing your web API. ASP.NET Web API is a framework that helps in building HTTP services that can be utilized by a wide range of clients. So it is very important to secure your Web API.

ASP.NET Web API 1.0 doesn't have any security features so the security is provided by the host such as Internet Information Server. In ASP.NET Web API 2, security features such as Katana were introduced. To secure Web API, let's understand various techniques that are involved and choose the right approach.

In this chapter, we will cover the following topics:

- ASP.NET Web API security architecture
- Setting up your browser client
- Authentication and authorization
- Implementing authentication in HTTP message handlers
- Setting the principal
- Using the [Authorize] Attribute
- Custom authorization filters
- Authorization inside a controller action

ASP.NET Web API security architecture

This section will give you an overview of the Web API security architecture and show you all the various extensibility points that can be used for security related things. The ASP.NET Web API security architecture is composed of three main layers. The hosting layer acts as an interface between the Web API and network stacks. The message handler pipeline layer enables implementing cross-cutting concerns such as authentication and caching. The controller handling layer is where the controllers and actions are executed, parameters are bound and validated, and HTTP response message is created. This layer also contains a filter pipeline, as shown in the following figure:

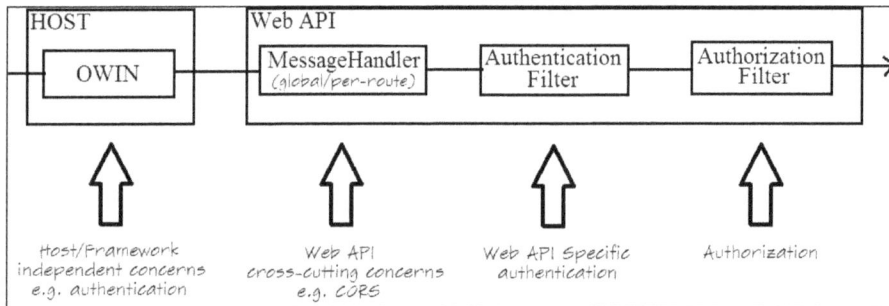

Fig 1 – This image shows the components involved in securing the Web API

Let's briefly discuss the purpose of each components in the Web API pipeline, as follows:

- **Open Web Interface for .NET (OWIN)** is the new open standard hosting infrastructure. Microsoft has built its own framework called Katana on top of OWIN and all Web API security techniques such as authentication methods (for example, token-based authentication) and support for social login providers (for example, Google and Facebook) will be happening on the OWIN layer.

- **Message Handler** is a class that receives an HTTP request and returns an HTTP response. Implementing authentication at message handler level is not recommended. Message handlers are used for **Cross-Origin Resource Sharing (CORS)**.

- **Authentication Filters** are guaranteed to run before the authorization filter. If you are not interested in operating your authentication logic at the OWIN layer, you can straightaway move to controllers or actions. Authentication filters are really useful to invoke OWIN-based authentication logic.

- **Authorization Filters** are the places in the pipeline where you can recheck the request before the actual expensive business logic stuff runs in the model binding and validation, and the controller action is invoked.

Now that we are familiar with the security architecture, we will set up the client.

Setting up your browser client

Let's create a Web API for Contact Lookup. This Contact Lookup Web API service will return the list of contacts to the calling client application. Then we will be consuming the Contact Lookup service using the jQuery AJAX call to list and search contacts.

This application will help us in demonstrating the Web API security throughout this book.

Implementing Web API lookup service

In this section, we are going to create a Contact Lookup web API service that returns a list of contacts in the **JavaScript Object Notation (JSON)** format. The client that consumes this Contact Lookup is a simple web page that displays the list of contacts using jQuery. Follow these steps to start the project:

1. Create **New Project** from the **Start** page in Visual Studio.

2. Select **Visual C# Installed Template** named **Web**.

3. Select **ASP.NET Web Application** in the center pane.

4. Name the project ContactLookup and click **OK**, as shown in the following screenshot:

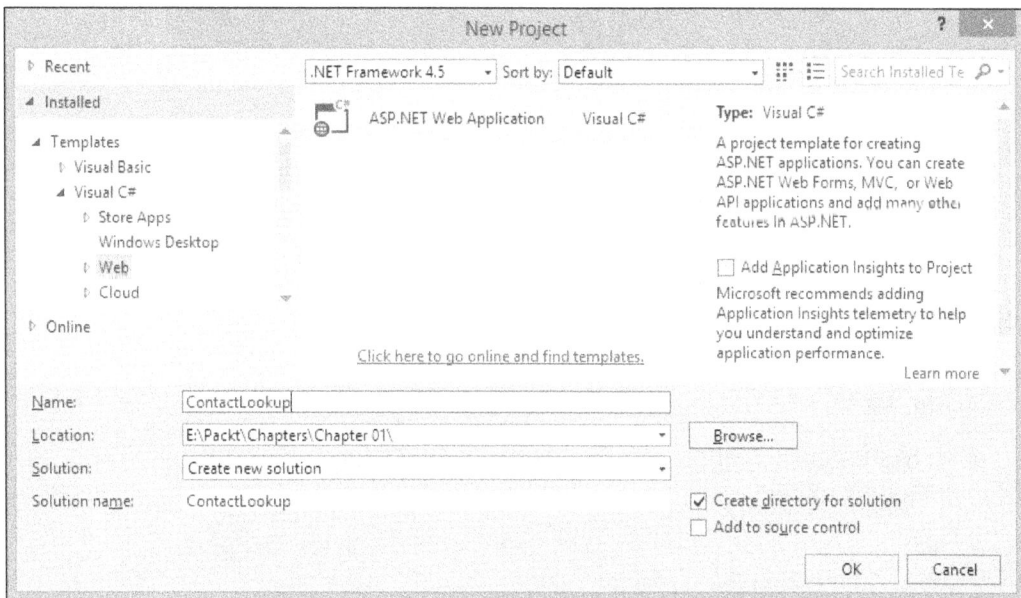

Fig 2 – We have named the ASP.NET Web Application "ContactLookup"

5. Select the **Empty** template in the **New ASP.NET Project** dialog box.

6. Check **Web API** and click **OK** under **Add folders and core references**, as shown in the following:

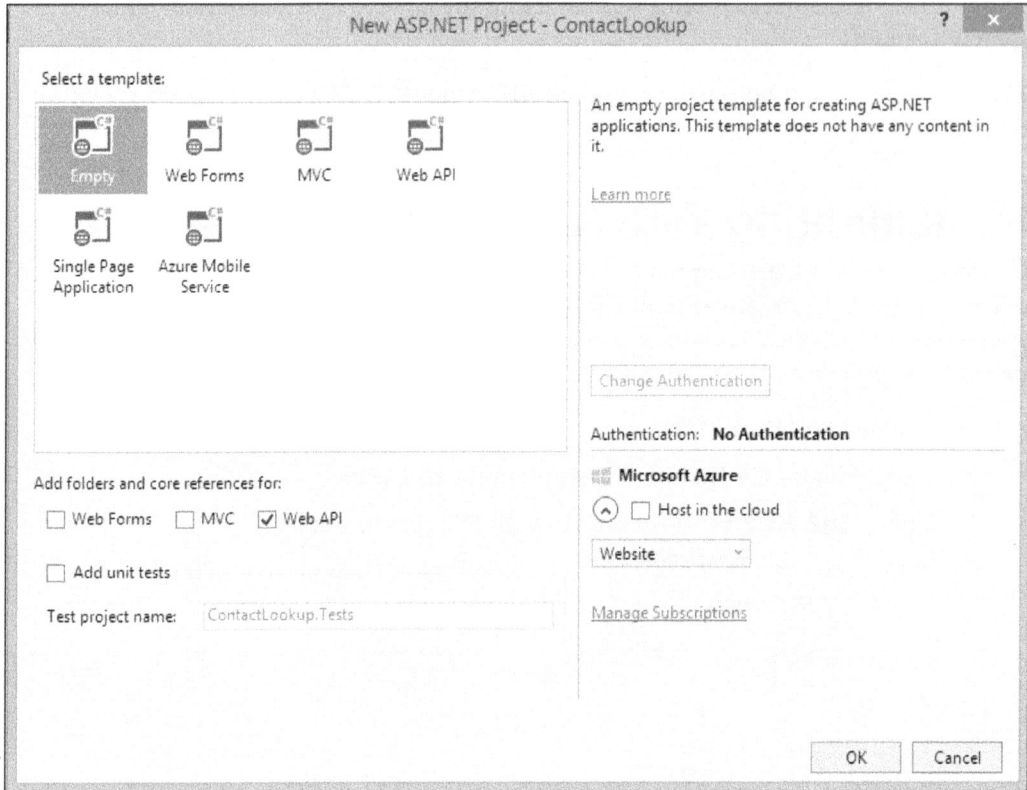

Fig 3 – We select the Empty Web API template

We just created an empty Web API project. Now let's add the required model.

Adding a model

Let's start by creating a simple model that represents a contact with the help of the following steps:

1. First, define a simple contact model by adding a class file to the **Models** folder.

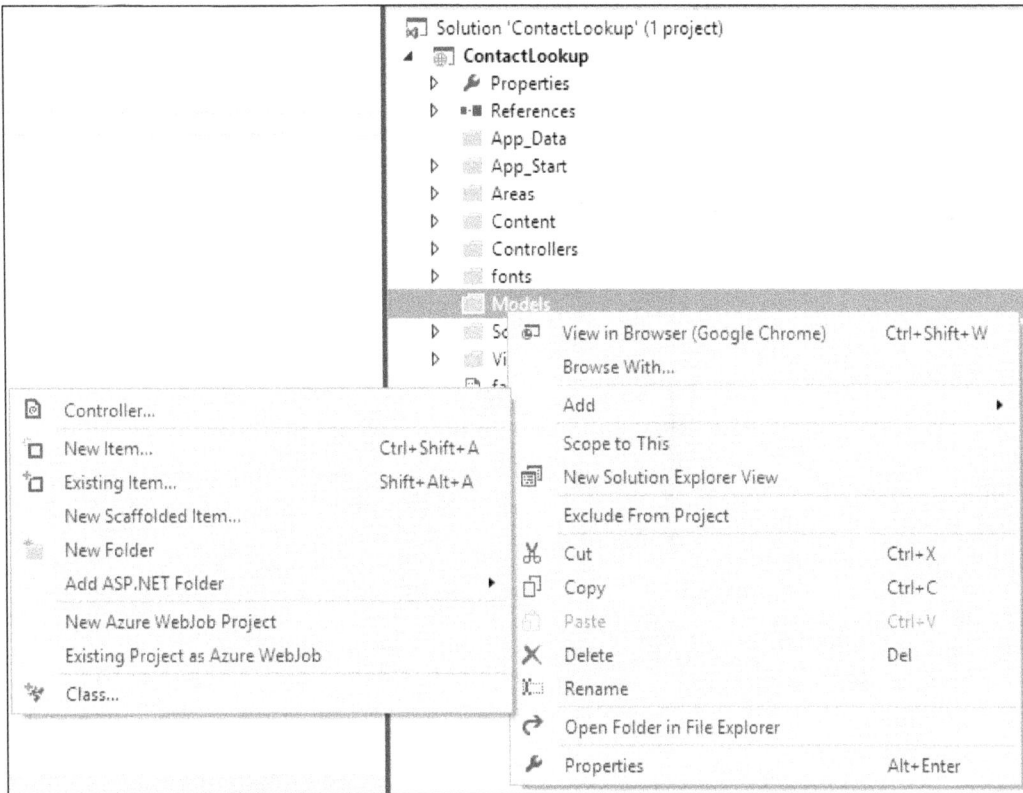

Fig 4 – Right-click on the Models folder and Add a Model Class

2. Name the class file `Contact` and declare properties of the `Contact` class.

```
namespace ContactLookup.Models
{
    public class Contact
    {
        public int Id { get; set; }
        public string Name { get; set; }
        public string Email { get; set; }
        public string Mobile { get; set; }
    }
}
```

We just added a model named `Contact`. Let's now add the required web API controller.

Adding a controller

HTTP requests are handled by controller objects in Web API. Let's define a controller with two action methods. One action to return the list of contacts and other action to return a single contact specific to a given ID:

1. Add the **Controller** under the **Controllers** folder in **Solution Explorer**.

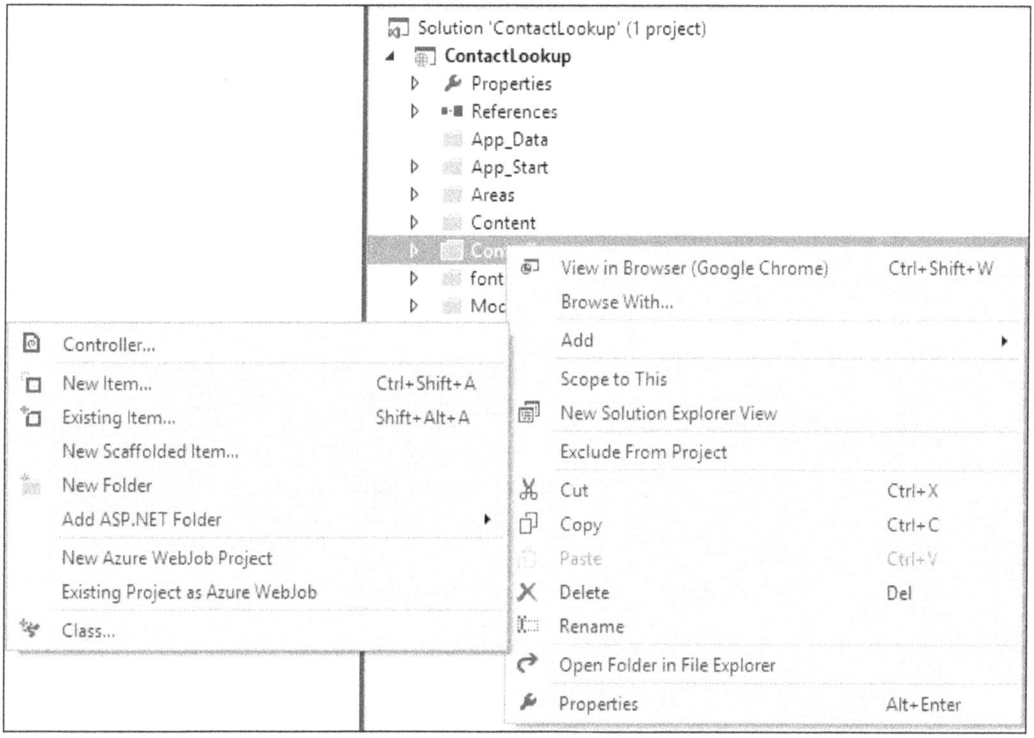

Fig 5 – Right-click on the Controllers folder and Add a Controller

2. Select **Web API Controller – Empty** and click on **Add** in the **Add Scaffold** dialog.

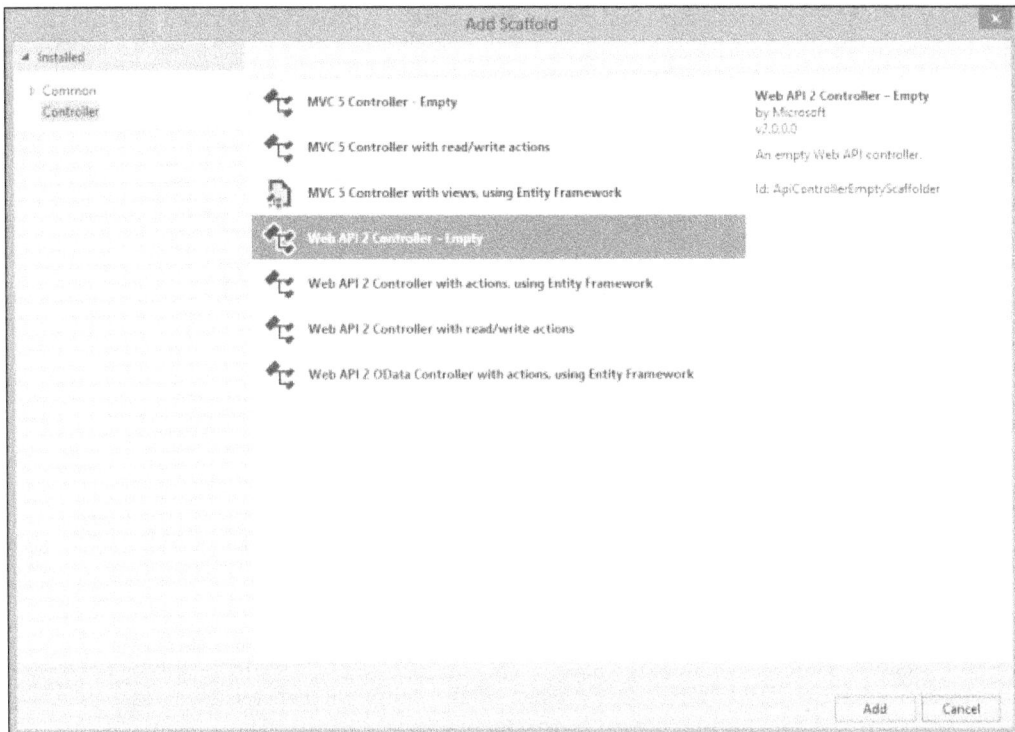

Fig 6 – Select an Empty Web API Controller

3. Let's name the controller `ContactsController` in the **Add Controller** dialog box and click **Add**.

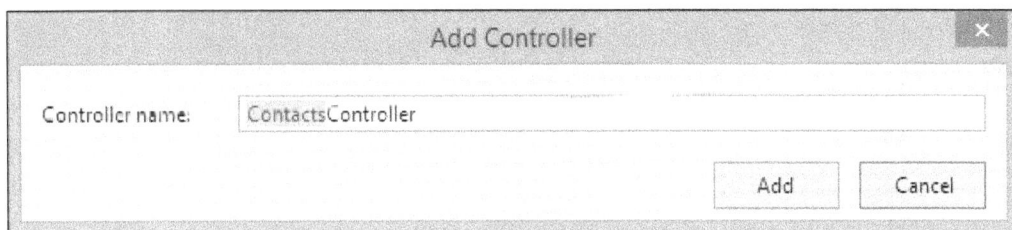

Fig 7 – Naming the controller

This creates the `ContactsController.cs` file in the **Controllers** folder as shown in the following image:

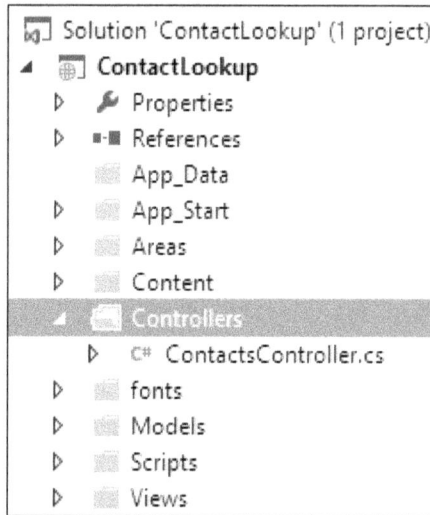

Fig 8 – ContactsController is added to the Controllers folder in the application

1. Replace the code in `ContactsController` with the following code:

```
namespace ContactLookup.Controllers
{
    public class ContactsController : ApiController
    {
        Contact[] contacts = new Contact[]
        {
            new Contact { Id = 1, Name = "Steve", Email = "steve@
gmail.com", Mobile = "+1(234)35434" },
            new Contact { Id = 2, Name = "Matt", Email = "matt@
gmail.com", Mobile = "+1(234)5654" },
            new Contact { Id = 3, Name = "Mark", Email = "mark@
gmail.com", Mobile = "+1(234)56789" }
        };

        public IEnumerable<Contact> GetAllContacts()
        {
            return contacts;
        }
```

```
public IHttpActionResult GetContact(int id)
{
    var contact = contacts.FirstOrDefault(x => x.Id ==
id);
    if (contact == null)
    {
        return NotFound();
    }
    return Ok(contact);
}
}
}
```

For simplicity, contacts are stored in a fixed array inside the controller class. The controller is defined with two action methods. List of contacts will be returned by the **GetAllContacts** method in the JSON format and the **GetContact** method returns a single contact by its ID. A unique URI is applied to each method on the controller as given in the following table:

Controller Method	URI
GetAllContacts	/api/contacts
GetContact	/api/contacts/id

Consuming the Web API using JavaScript and jQuery

In this section, in order to demonstrate calling the web API with or without any security mechanisms, let's create an HTML page that consumes web API and update the page with the results using the jQuery AJAX call:

1. In the **Solution Explorer** pane, right-click on the project and add **New Item**.

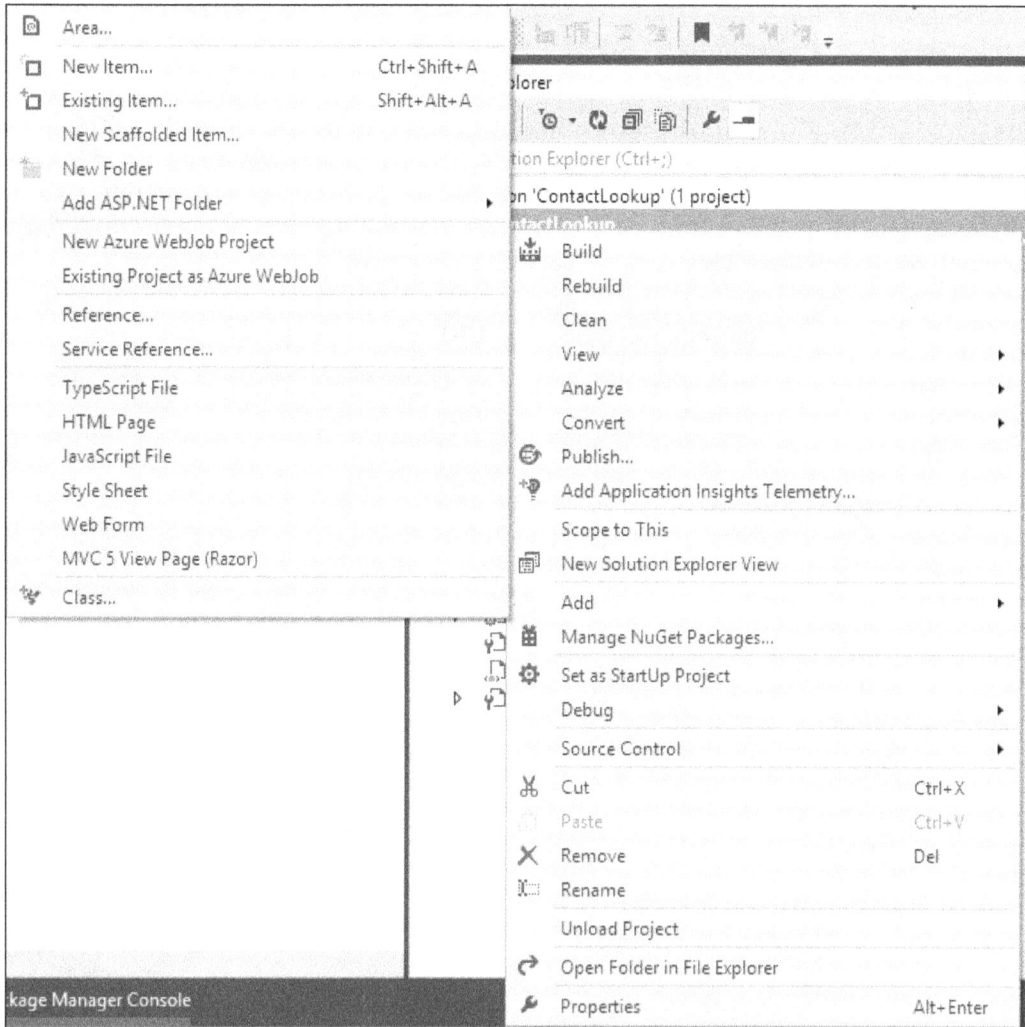

Fig 9 – Select add new item from the context menu in Solution Explorer

2. Create **HTML Page** named `index.html` using the **Add New Item** dialog.

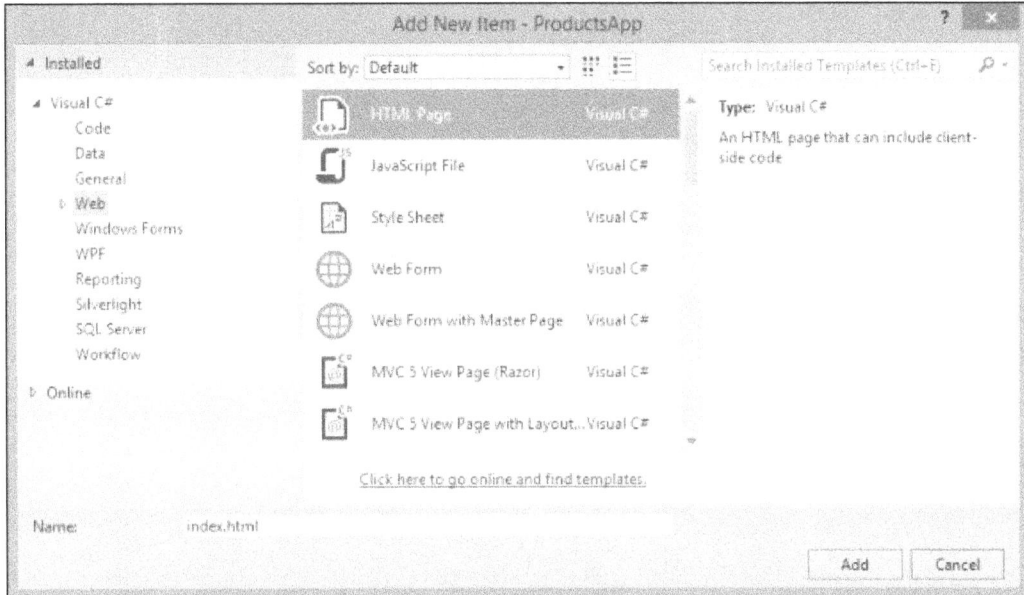

Fig 10 – Add an index html file by selecting HTML page in the Add New Item dialog

3. Replace the content of the `index.html` file with the following code:

```
<!DOCTYPE html>
<html xmlns="http://www.w3.org/1999/xhtml">
<head>
  <title>Contact Lookup</title>
</head>
<body>

  <div>
    <h2>All Contacts</h2>
    <ul id="contacts" />
  </div>
  <div>
    <h2>Search by ID</h2>
    <input type="text" id="contactId" size="5" />
    <input type="button" value="Search" onclick="search();" />
    <p id="contact" />
  </div>
```

```
  <script src="http://ajax.aspnetcdn.com/ajax/jQuery/jquery-
2.0.3.min.js"></script>
  <script>
    var uri = 'api/contacts';

    $(document).ready(function () {
      // Send an AJAX request
      $.getJSON(uri)
          .done(function (data) {
              // On success, 'data' contains a list of contacts.
              $.each(data, function (key, contact) {
                  // Add a list item for the contact.
                  $('<li>', { text: formatItem(contact)
}).appendTo($('#contacts'));
              });
          });
    });


function formatItem(contact) {
            return contact.Name + ', email: ' + contact.Email + ',
mobile: ' + contact.Mobile;
}

    function search() {
      var id = $('#contactId').val();
      $.getJSON(uri + '/' + id)
          .done(function (data) {
            $('#contact').text(formatItem(data));
          })
          .fail(function (jqXHR, textStatus, err) {
            $('#contact').text('Error: ' + err);
          });
    }
  </script>
</body>
</html>
```

Getting a list of contacts

We need to send an HTTP GET request to /api/contacts to get the list of contacts. The AJAX request is sent by the jQuery getJSON function and the array of JSON objects is received in the response. A callback function in the done function is called if the request succeeds. In the callback, we update the DOM with the contact information, as follows:

```
$(document).ready(function () {
    // Send an AJAX request
    $.getJSON(uri)
        .done(function (data) {
            // On success, 'data' variable contains a list of
contacts.
            $.each(data, function (key, contact) {
                // Add a list item for the contact.
                $('<li>', { text: formatItem(contact)
}).appendTo($('#contacts'));
            });
        });
    });
```

Getting a contact by ID

To get a contact by ID, send an HTTP GET request to /api/contacts/id, where id is the contact ID.

```
function search() {
    var id = $('#contactId').val();
    $.getJSON(uri + '/' + id)
        .done(function (data) {
            $('#contact').text(formatItem(data));
        })
        .fail(function (jqXHR, textStatus, err) {
            $('#contact').text('Error: ' + err);
        });
}
```

The request URL in getJSON has the contact ID. The response is a JSON representation of a single contact for this request.

Running the application

Start debugging the application by pressing *F5*. To search for a contact by ID, enter the ID and click on **Search**:

Fig 11 – User Interface of the Sample Browser-based Client Application

Authentication and authorization

We have created a simple web API that returns the list of contacts or specific contacts by ID. This web API can be accessed by any client that supports HTTP and is not secured enough. With the help of authentication and authorization mechanisms, we can secure this web API from unauthorized access.

- **Authentication** mechanism helps in identifying the valid user and authenticating them using the identity of the user. Here, the identity can be a username and password.

- **Authorization** mechanism helps in restricting unauthorized access to an action. For example, An unauthorized user can get the list of contacts. But he is restricted to create new contact.

Authentication

Authentication is carried out in the host **Internet Information Service (IIS)** for web API. Internet Information Service uses HTTP modules for authentication. We can also implement custom authentication with our own HTTP module.

The host creates a principal when it authenticates the user. Principal is an `IPrincipal` object that represents the security context under which the code is running. You can access the current principal from `Thread.CurrentPrincipal`, which is attached by the host. The user information can be accessed from the `Identity` object of principal. The `Identity.IsAuthenticated` property returns *true* if the user is authenticated. The `Identity.IsAuthenticated` will return *false* if the user is not authenticated.

Authorization

Authorization happens after successful authentication is provided to the controller. It helps you to grant access to resources when more granular choices are made.

For any unauthorized requests, the authorization filter returns an error response and does not allow the action to be executed. This happens as the authorization filters will be executed first before any statements in the controller action.

Implementing authentication in HTTP message handlers

For a self-hosted web API, the best practice is to implement authentication in an **HTTP Message Handler**. The principal will be set by the message handler after verifying the HTTP request. For a web API that is self-hosted, consider implementing authentication in a message handler. Otherwise, use an HTTP module instead.

The following code snippet shows an example of basic authentication implemented in an HTTP module:

```
public class AuthenticationHandler : DelegatingHandler
    {
        protected override Task<HttpResponseMessage>
SendAsync(HttpRequestMessage request,

CancellationToken cancellationToken)
        {
            var credentials = ParseAuthorizationHeader(request);

            if (credentials != null)
            {
                // Check if the username and passowrd in credentials
are valid against the ASP.NET membership.
                // If valid, the set the current principal in the
request context
```

```
                    var identity = new GenericIdentity(credentials.
Username);
                Thread.CurrentPrincipal = new
GenericPrincipal(identity, null);;
            }

        return base.SendAsync(request, cancellationToken)
            .ContinueWith(task =>
            {
                var response = task.Result;
                if (credentials == null && response.StatusCode ==
HttpStatusCode.Unauthorized)
                    Challenge(request, response);

                return response;
            });
        }

    protected virtual Credentials ParseAuthorizationHeader(HttpReq
uestMessage request)
        {
        string authorizationHeader = null;
        var authorization = request.Headers.Authorization;
        if (authorization != null && authorization.Scheme ==
"Basic")
            authorizationHeader = authorization.Parameter;

        if (string.IsNullOrEmpty(authorizationHeader))
            return null;

        authorizationHeader = Encoding.Default.GetString(Convert.
FromBase64String(authorizationHeader));

        var authenticationTokens = authorizationHeader.Split(':');
        if (authenticationTokens.Length < 2)
            return null;

        return new Credentials() { Username =
authenticationTokens[0], Password = authenticationTokens[1], };
        }

    void Challenge(HttpRequestMessage request, HttpResponseMessage
response)
        {
```

```
            response.Headers.Add("WWW-Authenticate", string.
    Format("Basic realm=\"{0}\"", request.RequestUri.DnsSafeHost));
        }

        public class Credentials
        {
            public string Username { get; set; }
            public string Password { get; set; }
        }
    }
```

Setting the principal

If the application has the custom authentication logic implemented, then we must set the principal in two places:

- `Thread.CurrentPrincipal` is the standard way to set the thread's principal in .NET.

- `HttpContext.Current.User` is specific to ASP.NET.

The following code shows setting up the principal:

```
private void SetPrincipal(IPrincipal principal)
{
    Thread.CurrentPrincipal = principal;
    if (HttpContext.Current != null)
    {
        HttpContext.Current.User = principal;
    }
}
```

Using the [Authorize] attribute

`AuthorizeAttribute` will make sure if the user is authenticated or unauthenticated. Unauthorized error with HTTP status code 401 will be returned if the user is not authenticated and the corresponding action will not be invoked. Web API enables you to apply the filter in three ways. We can apply them at global level, or at the controller level, or at the individual action level.

Global authorization filter

To apply authorization filter for all Web API controllers, we need to add the `AuthorizeAttribute` filter to the global filter list in the `Global.asax` file as given below:

```
public static void Register(HttpConfiguration config)
{
    config.Filters.Add(new AuthorizeAttribute());
}
```

Controller level authorization filter

To apply an authorization filter for a specific controller, we need to decorate the controller with filter attribute as given in the following code:

```
// Require authorization for all actions on the controller.
[Authorize]
public class ContactsController : ApiController
{
    public IEnumerable<Contact> GetAllContacts() { ... }
    public IHttpActionResult GetContact(int id) { ... }
}
```

Action level authorization filter

To apply an authorization filter for specific actions, we need to add the attribute to the action method as given in the following code:

```
public class ContactsController : ApiController
{
    public IEnumerable<Contact> GetAllContacts() { ... }

    // Require authorization for a specific action.
    [Authorize]
    public IHttpActionResult GetContact(int id) { ... }
}
```

Custom authorization filters

To implement a custom authorization filter, we need to create a class that derives either `AuthorizeAttribute`, `AuthorizationFilterAttribute`, or `IAuthorizationFilter`.

- `AuthorizeAttribute`: An action is authorized based on the current user and the user's roles.

- `AuthorizationFilterAttribute`: Synchronous authorization logic is applied and it may not be based on the current user or role.

- `IAuthorizationFilter`: Both `AuthorizeAttribute` and `AuthorizationFilterAttribute` implement `IAuthorizationFilter`. `IAuthorizationFilter` is to be implemented if advanced authorization logic is required.

Authorization inside a controller action

Sometimes, it may be required to change the behavior after processing the request based on the principal. In such scenarios, we can implement authorization in a controller action. For example, if you would like to manipulate the response based on the user's role, we can verify the logged-in user role from the `ApiController.User` property in the action method itself:

```
public HttpResponseMessage Get()
{
    if (!User.IsInRole("Admin"))
    {
        // manipulate the response to eliminate information that
shouldn't be shared with non admin users
    }
}
```

Summary

That was easy, wasn't it? We just set up the security for our APS.NET Web API that we will build upon in the upcoming chapters.

You learned about the security architecture of ASP.NET Web API that gave an overall view of what's under the hood. We then set up our browser client, from implementing the Web lookup service to calling the Web API with JavaScript and jQuery code.

You also learned about authentication and authorization techniques, which we will be covering in great detail later in the book. Moving on, you learned about HTTP Message Handlers, Principal, and the [Authorize] Attribute to control the authorization for the users.

Finally, you learned about custom authorization and authorization in a controller action to alter the behavior after processing the request based on the principal.

You learned a lot of stuff in this chapter. However, this is just the beginning. In the next chapter, you will implement a secured socket layer to the Web API. Let's get the ball rolling!

2
Enabling SSL for ASP.NET Web API

In this chapter, we will discuss the implementation of SSL with ASP.NET Web API and authentication of users using SSL client certificates. Authentication schemes over plain HTTP are not secure. For example, basic authentication and forms authentication send plain texts, such as the username and password. So, to protect the plain texts from vulnerability, we use SSL and also authenticate clients using the SSL client certificates.

In this chapter, we will cover the following topics:

- Enforcing SSL in a Web API controller
- Using Client certificates in Web API

Enforcing SSL in a Web API controller

The **Secure Sockets Layer** (**SSL**) encryption protects the credentials exchanged between a client and a server. SSL enables a secure channel to transfer authentication messages in an encrypted format. The 128-bit and 256-bit SSL encryption techniques are more secure. Required 128-bit or 256-bit SSL is used if confidential or personal data is to be transmitted between a client and server. It is very difficult to decrypt the content that is encrypted using the 128-bit or 256-bit encryption technique.

SSL and **Transport Level Security** (**TLS**) use a combination of public key and symmetric key encryption. The SSL handshake is an exchange of messages during the initial communication between the server and client. Using public-key techniques allows the server to authenticate itself to the client during this handshake process.

RSA is a key exchange algorithm that governs the way the server and client determine the symmetric keys to use during an SSL handshake. The SSL cipher suites use an RSA key exchange and the TLS supports the ECC cipher suites and RSA.

OpenSSH is based on the SSH protocol and it helps in securing the network communication through network traffic encryption over multiple authentication methods and by providing secure tunneling capabilities. OpenSSH is a free and open source that can be used as an alternative to the unencrypted network communication protocols like FTP and Rlogin.

Enabling SSL allows the clients to access the site using the URLs that start with HTTPS. We can create Self-Signed Certificates in IIS 7 or later versions; it can be used to enable SSL for a site and add an HTTPS binding. For development purpose, we can enable SSL in IIS Express from Visual Studio and set **SSL Enabled** to **True** in the **Properties** window, as shown in the following screenshot:

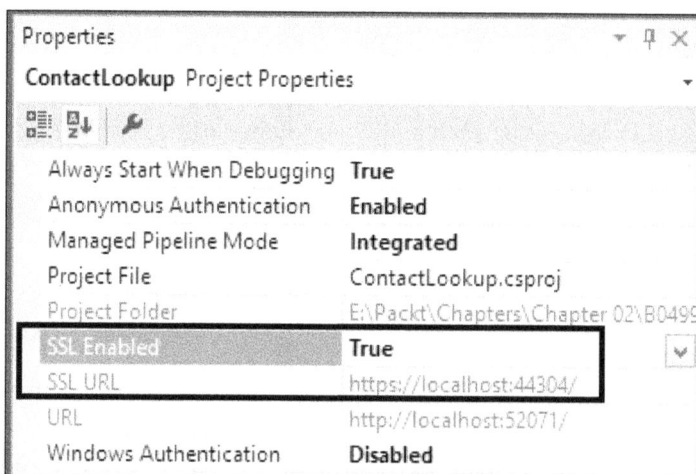

In some situations, we may want to support both HTTPS and HTTP binding. We can enable HTTP for some resources or actions and SSL for others. In such cases, we can add the actions with the `RequireHttps` filter attribute to required SSL. The following code is a Web API authentication filter that verifies for SSL:

```
public class RequireHttpsAttribute : AuthorizationFilterAttribute
{
    public override void OnAuthorization(HttpActionContext
actionContext)
    {
        if (actionContext.Request.RequestUri.Scheme != Uri.
UriSchemeHttps)
        {
```

```
        actionContext.Response = new HttpResponseMessage(System.
Net.HttpStatusCode.Forbidden)
            {
                ReasonPhrase = "HTTPS Required"
            };
        }
        else
        {
            base.OnAuthorization(actionContext);
        }
    }
}
```

As shown in the following, you can add any Web API action that requires SSL with the `RequireHttps` filter:

```
public class ContactsController : ApiController
{
    [RequireHttps]
    public IEnumerable<Contact> GetAllContacts() { ... }
}
```

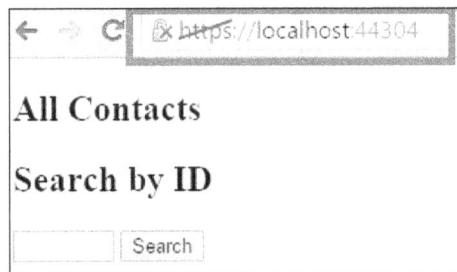

Using client certificates in Web API

To digitally identify whether a user is an authenticated user, client certificates are used. This is an enhanced security mechanism unlike using username and password for security as this is a simple validation. Client certificates allow a web application to authenticate its users by verifying a certificate that is provided by the client before the HTTP connection is established.

Creating an SSL Client Certificate

The following steps will create a test root authority and client certification for development and testing purpose:

1. Open Developer Command Prompt for Visual Studio.

2. Run the following command:

   ```
   makecert.exe -n "CN=Dev CA" -r -sv DevCA.pvk DevCA.cer
   ```

3. Enter the certificate password when prompted by `makecert` for private key.

The preceding steps help in creating the Root Certification Authority certificate. Now let's install the `DevCA.cer` certificate on our Trusted Root Certification Authorities for the local machine store using **Microsoft Management Control (MMC)** by following the steps:

1. Open Microsoft Management Control.

2. Click on **Add/Remove Snap-in** from the **File** menu.

3. Select **Certificates** from the list of **Available snap-ins** and click on the **Add** button.

4. Choose **Computer Account** from the **Certificates snap-in** popup to manage certificates and click on the **Next** button.

5. Select **Local Computer** in the **Select Computer** window and click on the **Finish** button.

6. Now click on **OK** to return to MMC.

7. Under the **Console Root** tree view, select the **Trusted Root Certification Authorities** node.

8. Click on **More Actions** in the **Actions** pane and navigate to **All Tasks | Import** to import certificate.

9. Browse for the `DevCA.cer` certificate file and click on the **Open** button.

10. Click on **Next** and complete the wizard.

11. Re-enter the password when prompted.

12. Execute the following command in Developer Command Prompt for Visual Studio to create a signed client certificate:

    ```
    makecert.exe -pe -ss My -sr CurrentUser -a sha1 -sky exchange -n
    "CN=name" -eku 1.3.6.1.5.5.7.3.2 -sk SignedByCA -ic DevCA.cer -iv
    DevCA.pvk
    ```

Configuring IIS to accept client certificates

The following steps will configure IIS to accept client certificates:

1. Click on the site node in the tree view of IIS Manager.
2. Open the **SSL Settings** by double-clicking on it.
3. Select any one of these options in **Client Certificates**:
   - **Accept**: IIS will accept a certificate from the client but does not require one
   - **Require**: IIS requires a client certificate (To enable this option, you must also select **Require SSL**)

Now you know how to configure in order to accept or require client certificates in IIS Express. Next, we will see how to use client certificates in Web API.

Verifying Client Certificates in Web API

Enabling HTTPS and using the client certificates with SSL and distributing the signed certificates to the users will secure Web API and authenticate the client.

Calling `GetClientCertificate` on the request message returns the client certificate to Web API. The method returns null if there is no client certificate. The `X509Certificate2` instance will be returned if there is a client certificate. We can get details about the issuer and subject from the `X509Certificate2` instance object, and it can be used for authentication and authorization:

```
X509Certificate2 cert = Request.GetClientCertificate();
string issuer = cert.Issuer;
string subject = cert.Subject;
```

Summary

We just saw how to use SSL with ASP.NET Web API and learned how to implement the basic authentication and forms authentication using SSL.

You also learned about creating client certificates and configuring IIS to accept them.

You got to know how to use client certificates in Web API.

In the next chapter, let's integrate the ASP.NET Identity systems with the ASP.NET Web API. The ASP.NET Identity systems will help you to implement social logins to your application. It also enables you to store the user profile information such as dates of birth. ASP.NET Identity is available in ASP.NET MVC, Web Forms, and Web API templates.

3
Integrating ASP.NET Identity System with Web API

This chapter practically explains how to integrate ASP.NET Identity system with ASP.NET Web API. The ASP.NET Identity system is an upgrade to the ASP.NET Membership and Simple Membership systems. It has user profile support, OAuth integration and is available in the ASP.NET templates of Visual Studio 2013/2015.

In this chapter, we will cover the following topics:

- Creating an empty Web API application
- Installing the ASP.NET Identity NuGet packages
- Setting up the ASP.NET Identity 2.1
- Defining Web API controllers and methods

Creating an Empty Web API Application

Let's create an empty Web API to integrate ASP.NET Identity. Follow the given steps:

1. Create **New Project** from the **Start** page in Visual Studio.

2. Select **Visual C# Installed Template** named **Web**.

3. Select **ASP.NET Web Application** in the center pane.

4. Name the project `ContactLookupWithAspNetIdentity` and click on **OK**:

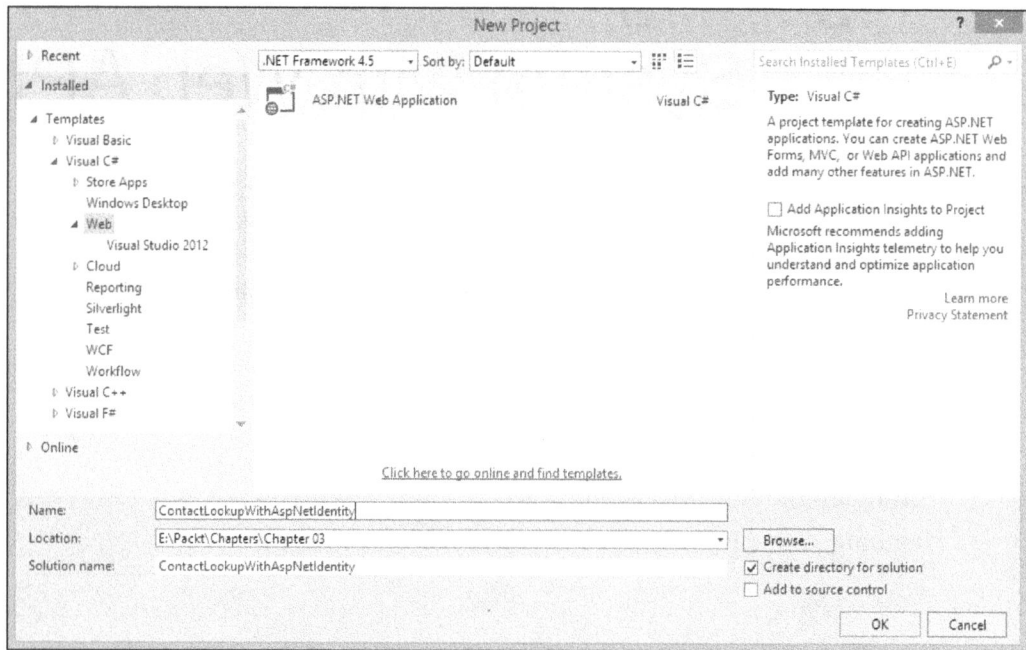

Fig 1 – We have named the ASP.NET Web Application as ContactLookupWithAspNetIdentity

5. Select the **Empty** template in the **New ASP.NET Project** dialog.

6. Check **Web API** and click **OK** under **Add folders and core references**:

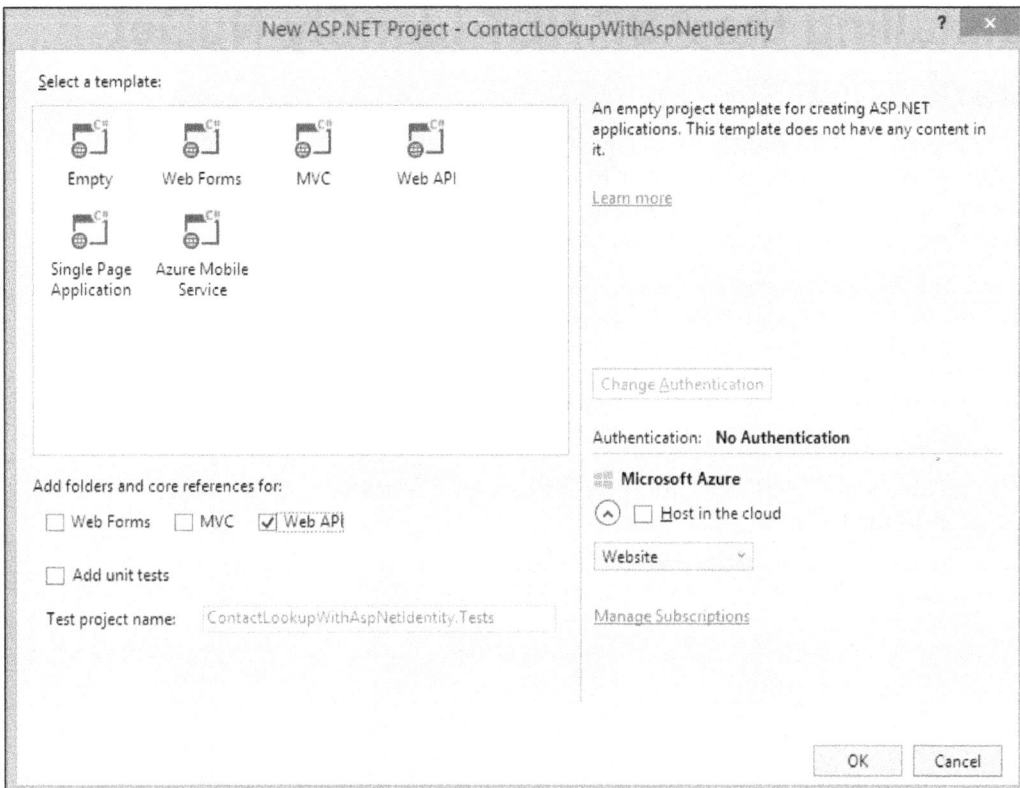

Fig 2 – Select ASP.NET Web API template for Application "ContactLookupWithAspNetIdentity"

The solution of the empty Web API that is created generates the following files:

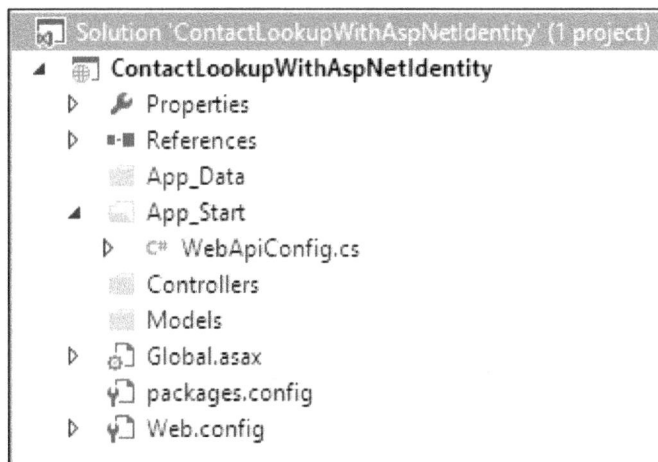

Fig 3 – Solution structure of empty ASP.NET Web API Application "ContactLookupWithAspNetIdentity"

Installing the ASP.NET Identity NuGet packages

We have created an Empty Web API Web Application. Now we need to install the required NuGet packages in order to integrate ASP.NET Identity into Web API. Let's execute the following statements under the NuGet package manager console to install the ASP.NET Identity 2.1 package to the created application:

```
Install-Package Microsoft.AspNet.Identity.Core
Install-Package Microsoft.AspNet.Identity.EntityFramework
Install-Package Microsoft.AspNet.Identity.OWIN
Install-Package Microsoft.OWIN.Cors
Install-Package Microsoft.AspNet.WebApi.OWIN
Install-Package Microsoft.OWIN.Security.OAuth
```

We can also install ASP.NET Identity 2.1 using a UI-based Nuget package manager as given in the following screenshot:

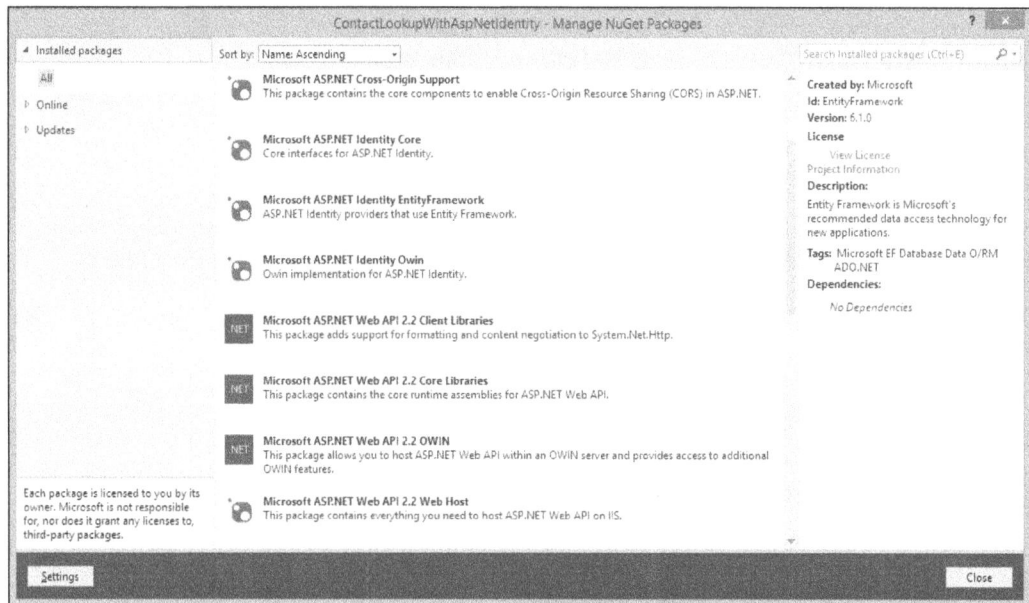

Fig 4 – Installing ASP.NET Identity 2.0 related packages using NuGet Package Manager

Setting up ASP.NET Identity 2.1

We have created an empty Web API and installed the necessary NuGet packages for ASP.NET Identity and **Open Web Interface for .Net (OWIN)**. Now let's add the required class files to integrate ASP.NET Identity into Web API.

ASP.NET Identity

ASP.NET Identity is a framework provided by Microsoft that was created on top of OWIN middleware to manage user identity and membership in ASP.NET applications such as Web Forms, MVC, and Web API. We are going to use the ASP.NET Identity system to register and manage identity users using the in-built domain model for identity user called IdentityUser. If you are planning to have extra properties in your application, then you would need to create a domain model with extra properties inheriting IdentityUser. Let's define a custom entity framework class with application-specific properties for user, such as first name and last name. We also need to define a db context that will handle the communication with the database:

1. Let's create a class named ApplicationUser inheriting IdentityUser in the Models folder:

    ```
    public class ApplicationUser : IdentityUser
    {
        [Required]
        [MaxLength(50)]
        public string FirstName { get; set; }

        [Required]
        [MaxLength(50)]
        public string LastName { get; set; }
    }
    ```

    This extended identity user class contains application-specific extra properties, such as the FirstName and LastName data, annotated with the required and maximum length validation attributes.

2. Now, add a class named ApplicationDbContext to the Models folder to manage communication with db:

    ```
    public class ApplicationDbContext : IdentityDbContext<ApplicationU
    ser>
    {
      public ApplicationDbContext()
      : base("DefaultConnection", throwIfV1Schema: false)
      {
      Configuration.ProxyCreationEnabled = false;
      Configuration.LazyLoadingEnabled = false;
      }

      public static ApplicationDbContext Create()
      {
      return new ApplicationDbContext();
      }
    }
    ```

We just created an `ApplicationDbContext` class file inheriting `IdentityDbContext` that will help to manage the identity-specific tables in SQL Server. As you can see, we are passing the connection string name as a parameter to base constructor so that it can be used to identify the respective server and database names.

3. Let's now add the connection string to the `web.config` file that will point to the database, which will be created using code first approach:

```
<connectionStrings>
    <add name="DefaultConnection" connectionString="(LocalDb)\v11.
0;AttachDbFilename=|DataDirectory|\AspNetIdentity.mdf;Initial Cata
log=AspNetIdentity;Integrated Security=True" providerName="System.
Data.SqlClient" />
</connectionStrings>
```

We added the required connection string. Now, we need to enable the entity framework code first migration that will generate the code in order to update the database schema from the domain model code.

4. To add the NuGet package for migration, execute the following commands in the NuGet Package Manager Console:

```
enable-migrations
add-migration AspNetDbCreate
update-database
```

   ° The `enable-migrations` command creates the `Migrations` folder in the `ContactLookupWithAspNetIdentity` project and generates a file named `Configuration`. The `Seed` method adds the basic data to db that is required to run or test the application.

   ° The `add-migration AspNetDbCreate` command generates the `<timestamp>_AspNetDbCreate.cs` code in the `Migrations` folder to create database. If you notice, the file also contains the code for the extended application-specific data properties in the `ApplicationUser` class in method `Up`.

   ° The `update-database` command executes the code in the `Up` method and the code in the `Seed` method in the `<timestamp>_AspNetDbCreate.cs` configuration file.

The following image shows the solution structure after adding the required files and enabling migration:

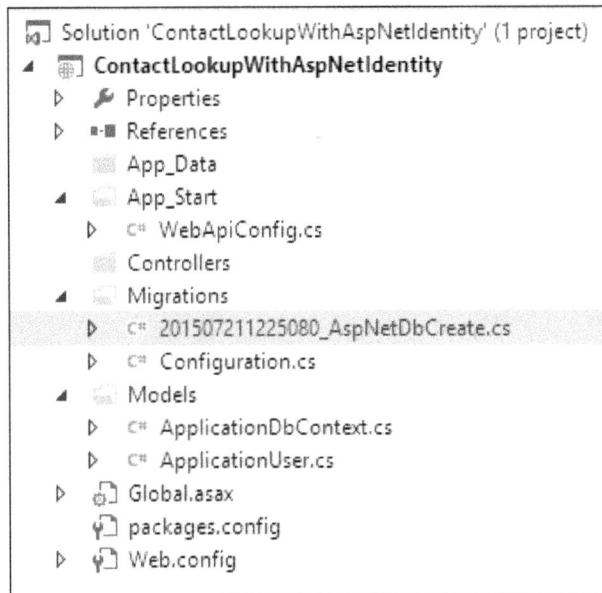

Fig 5 – Solution structure of "ContactLookupWithAspNetIdentity" with Db Migration configuration file

1. Add the `UserManager` class to manage `ApplicationUser` instances. To do this, let's create a file named `IdentityConfig.cs` in `App_Start` as a standard, and add the following code for the `UserManager` class to it:

```
public class ApplicationUserManager : UserManager<ApplicationUser>
{
    public ApplicationUserManager(IUserStore<ApplicationUser>
store) : base(store)
    {
    }

    public static ApplicationUserManager Create(IdentityFactoryOpti
ons<ApplicationUserManager> options, IOWINContext context)
    {
    var appDbContext = context.Get<ApplicationDbContext>();
    var appUserManager = new ApplicationUserManager(new UserStore<Ap
plicationUser>(appDbContext));

    return appUserManager;
    }
}
```

We can also add code in the create method of the `ApplicationUserManager` class to configure validation logic for username and password, implement two-factor authentication providers for e-mail and SMS, and enable Role-based authorization for Web API.

The following code adds the rule to validate user profiles. As per the code, the usernames are restricted to accept only alphanumeric usernames (the usernames should start with alphabets) and the e-mail address should be valid and mandatory:

```
manager.UserValidator = new UserValidator<ApplicationUser>(manager)
{
    AllowOnlyAlphanumericUserNames = true,
    RequireUniqueEmail = true
};
```

The following code adds the rule to validate passwords to restrict the password's minimum and maximum length and to consist of at least one special character, a digit, and at least one upper or lower case letter:

```
manager.PasswordValidator = new PasswordValidator
{
    RequiredLength = 6,
    RequireNonLetterOrDigit = true,
    RequireDigit = true,
    RequireLowercase = true,
    RequireUppercase = true,
};
```

The static `Create` method in the `ApplicationUserManager` class will be registered in `Startup.Auth.cs` as a callback method that will be invoked in order to create an instance of `ApplicationUserManager`. This instance will be stored in `OWINContext` and is available by calling the `context.Get` method:

Add the OWIN Startup class with the following code to the `App_Start` folder:

```
public partial class Startup
{

    public void Configuration(IAppBuilder app)
    {
    HttpConfiguration httpConfig = new HttpConfiguration();

    ConfigureOAuthTokenGeneration(app);

    ConfigureWebApi(httpConfig);
```

```
    app.UseCors(Microsoft.OWIN.Cors.CorsOptions.AllowAll);

    app.UseWebApi(httpConfig);

    }

    private void ConfigureOAuthTokenGeneration(IAppBuilder app)
    {
    app.CreatePerOWINContext(ApplicationDbContext.Create);
       app.CreatePerOWINContext<ApplicationUserManager>
(ApplicationUserManager.Create);
    }

    private void ConfigureWebApi(HttpConfiguration config)
    {
    config.MapHttpAttributeRoutes();

    var jsonFormatter = config.Formatters.OfType<JsonMediaTypeFormat
ter>().First();
    jsonFormatter.SerializerSettings.ContractResolver = new
CamelCasePropertyNamesContractResolver();
    }
}
```

This Startup class provides you with the ability to configure the authorization information and the Web API HTTP, set up the accessibility of CORS, JSON type formatter, and so on.

The application user manager instance is made available in the account controller by injecting to the constructor or from OWINContext in the Request object. The instance of application user manager provides methods to get identity the user information, change the password, add external login information for the identity user, remove local or external login of an identity user, register a user, and add the login information.

Defining Web API Controllers and methods

So far, we created an empty ASP.NET Web API application. We installed the necessary NuGet packages for ASP.NET Identity and OWIN integration. We also added the code for identity user and db context, and enabled the db migration for the entity framework code first migration. Now let's add the required controllers and methods to manage user accounts in application identity system.

Create a controller named `AccountsController` and add the following code:

```
namespace ContactLookupWithAspNetIdentity.Controllers
{
    [RoutePrefix("api/accounts")]
    public class AccountsController : ApiController
    {
        public ApplicationUserManager UserManager
        {
            get
            {
                return Request.GetOWINContext().GetUserManager<Applica
tionUserManager>();
            }
        }

        [Route("user/{id:guid}")]
        public async Task<IHttpActionResult> GetUserById (string Id)
        {
            var user = await UserManager.FindByIdAsync(Id);
            if (user != null)
            {
                return Json(user);
            }

            return NotFound();
        }

        [Route("user/{username}")]
        public async Task<IHttpActionResult> GetUserByName(string
username)
        {
            var user = await UserManager.FindByNameAsync(username);

            if (user != null)
            {
                return Json(user);
            }
            return NotFound();

        }


    [HttpPost]
```

```
[Route("Register")]
public async Task<IHttpActionResult> Register([FromBody]
UserViewModel userVM)
{
    var user = new ApplicationUser() {
        UserName = userVM.UserName,
        Email = userVM.Email,
        FirstName = userVM.FirstName,
        LastName = userVM.LastName
    };

    IdentityResult result = await UserManager.
CreateAsync(user, "password@1");

    if (!result.Succeeded)
    {
        return InternalServerError();
    }

    return Ok();
}
}
}
```

There are three methods in `AccountsController` namely, `GetUserById`, `GetUserByName`, and `GetRegister`. Note that the `Register` method is implemented as `HttpPost` to accept the user instance from POST body and this identity user is inserted in the database. The `GetUserById` and `GetUserByName` methods will return user information that matches with the respective ID or name.

Testing the application

We just created the necessary controllers and methods in order to manage identity users for an application such as `ContactLookup`. Now, let's test `AccountsController` to verify that the implemented method to insert an identity user and get the identity user based on its ID or name works properly.

Let's first invoke the `Register` method using the `Fiddler` tool as given in the following screenshot:

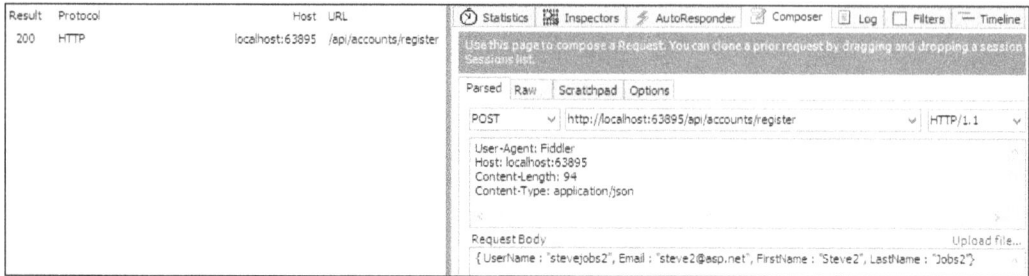

Fig 6 – POST user instance to ASP.NET Web API Register method in Accounts controller

As you can see, we posted user instance to the Web API `Register` method using the `POST` action via `Fiddler`:

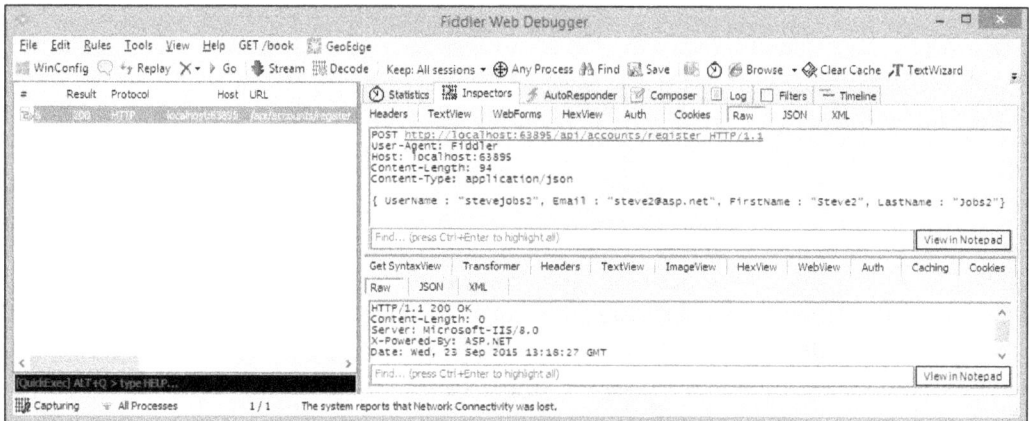

Fig 7 – 200 OK response indicating user has been created

The Web API returned a response with HTTP status code `200 OK`. This means that the new identity user has been created and inserted into the identity database, as shown in the following screenshot:

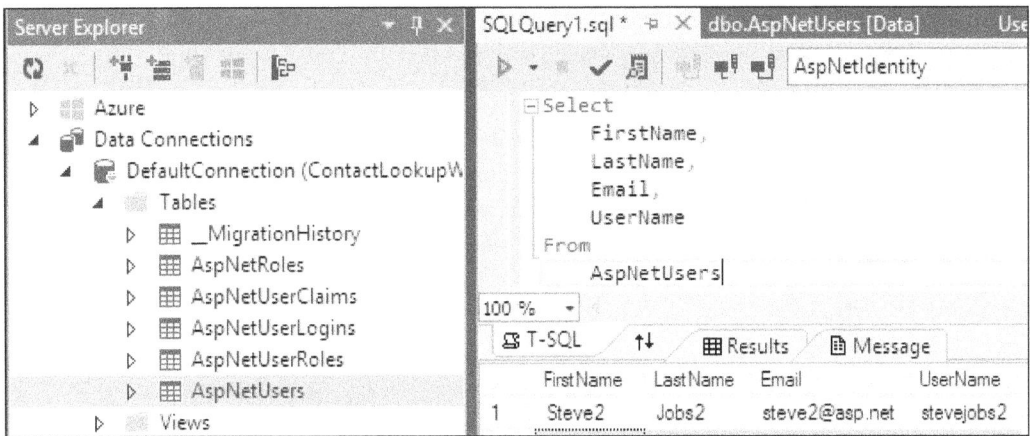

Fig 8 – Registered identity user is added to the database

Now, let's try to get the inserted user details by passing the user ID (a GUID) to the Web API action method, as shown in the following screenshot:

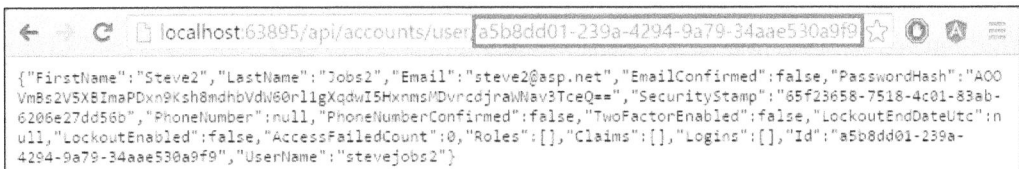

Fig 9 – Applying GET action to the User method passing user ID

As you can see, we applied the GET action to the URL appending the respective GUID of the identity user inserted and we received the user details in the XML/JSON format of the found matching user.

Now, let's try to get the inserted user details by passing the username to the Web API action method, as shown in the following screenshot:

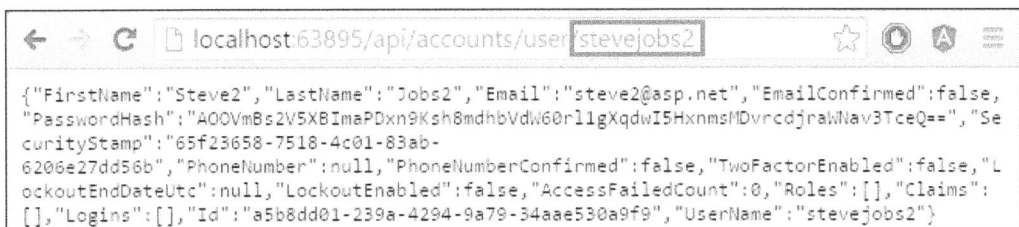

Fig 10 – Applying GET action to the User method passing username

Similarly, we have appended the username of the identity user to the URL by applying the GET method. The response contains the matching user details in the XML/JSON format.

Now, the Web API is ready with the ASP.NET Identity system integrated. So, it will be easy for us to manage the identity users using the built-in functionalities provided by the ASP.NET Identity system. Next, you can add LookupController with the necessary methods to return the details of the contacts.

Summary

That was easy, wasn't it? We just integrated APS.NET Identity with Web API in order to manage the identity user and membership.

You learned the step by step creation of an empty ASP.NET Web API project that is used to integrate ASP.NET Identity. We then installed the necessary ASP.NET Identity NuGet packages as a part of the integration process.

You also learned how to define controllers and methods in order to manage the identity user and membership for the application.

Finally, you learned about testing the ASP.NET Identity integration with an empty Web API created. Now, we have the necessary controllers and methods to manage application user for ContactLookup. Next, you can create other controllers that are required to enable search on the available contacts for the ContactLookup service.

You learned the ASP.NET Identity integration to Web API in this chapter. In the next chapter, you will secure Web API using OAuth2.

Let's get those security walls up!

4
Securing Web API Using OAuth2

This chapter explains how to secure a web API using OAuth2 to authenticate against a membership database using OWIN middleware. You will be able to use local logins to send authenticated requests using OAuth2.

In this chapter, we will cover the following topics:

- Host OWIN in IIS and add Web API to the OWIN pipeline
- Individual User Account Login authentication flow
- Send an unauthorized request
- Get an access token
- Send an authenticated request

Hosting OWIN in IIS and adding Web API to the OWIN pipeline

Let's create an empty Web API template to integrate ASP.NET Identity. Follow the given steps:

1. Create **New Project** from the **Start** page in Visual Studio.
2. Select **Visual C# Installed Template** named **Web**.
3. Select **ASP.NET Web Application** in the center pane.

4. Name the project `ContactLookupOwin` and click **OK**:

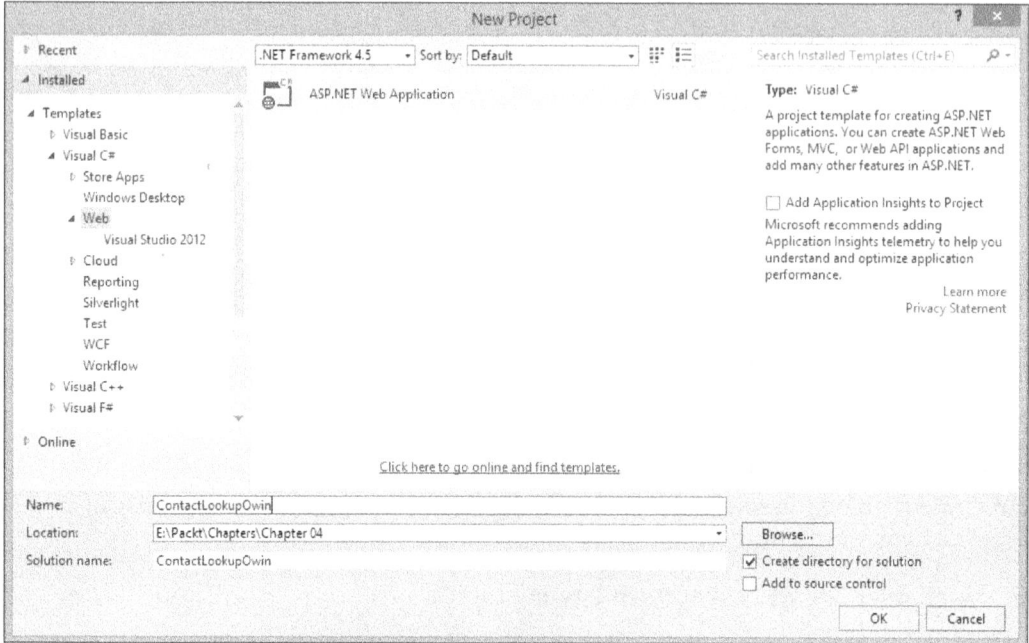

Fig 1 – We have named the ASP.NET Web Application as "ContactLookupOwin"

5. Select the **Empty** template in the **New ASP.NET Project** dialog and click **OK**:

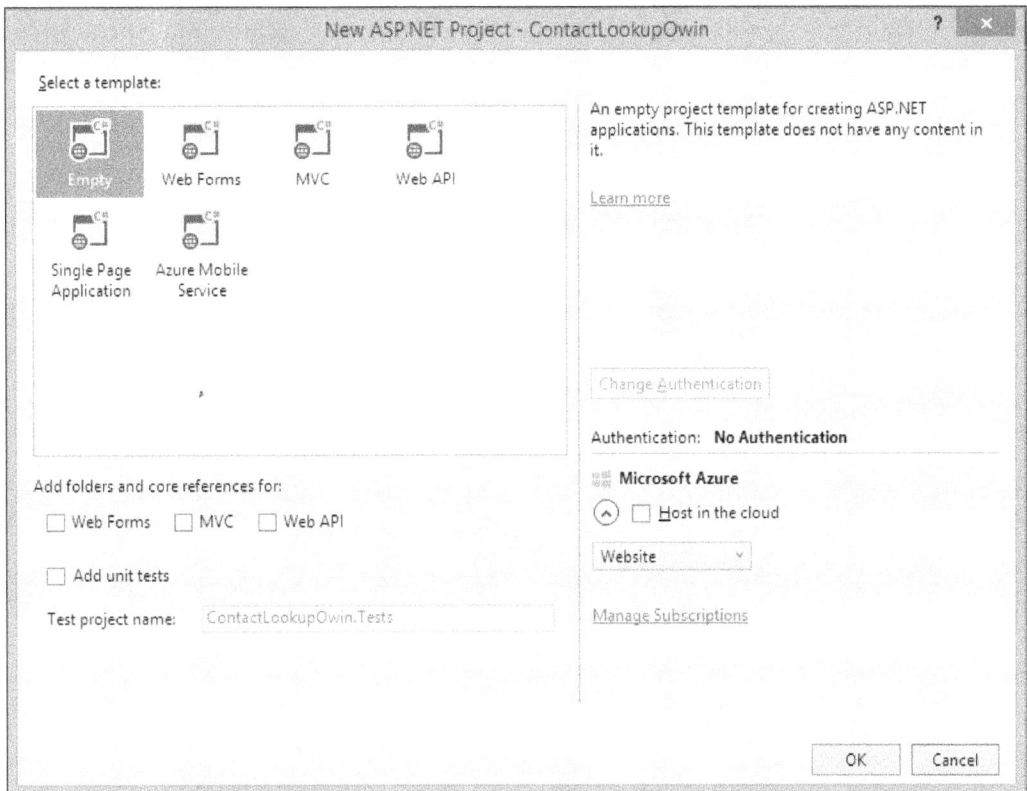

Fig 2 – Select Empty template for Application "ContactLookupOwin"

6. Install **NuGet packages** for the OWIN server that enables OWIN-based applications to run on IIS using the ASP.NET request pipeline:

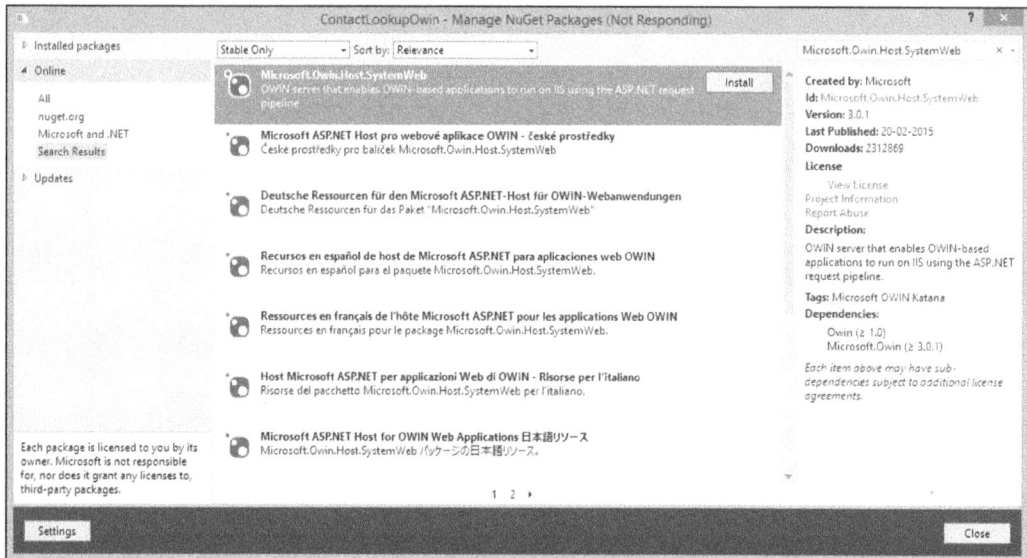

Fig 3 – Installed NuGet package "Microsoft.Owin.Host.SystemWeb"

7. Right-click on **Project** and select **Add New Item** in the `ContactLookupOwin` project. Then, select the OWIN startup class in the center pane and name the class file `OwinStartup.cs`:

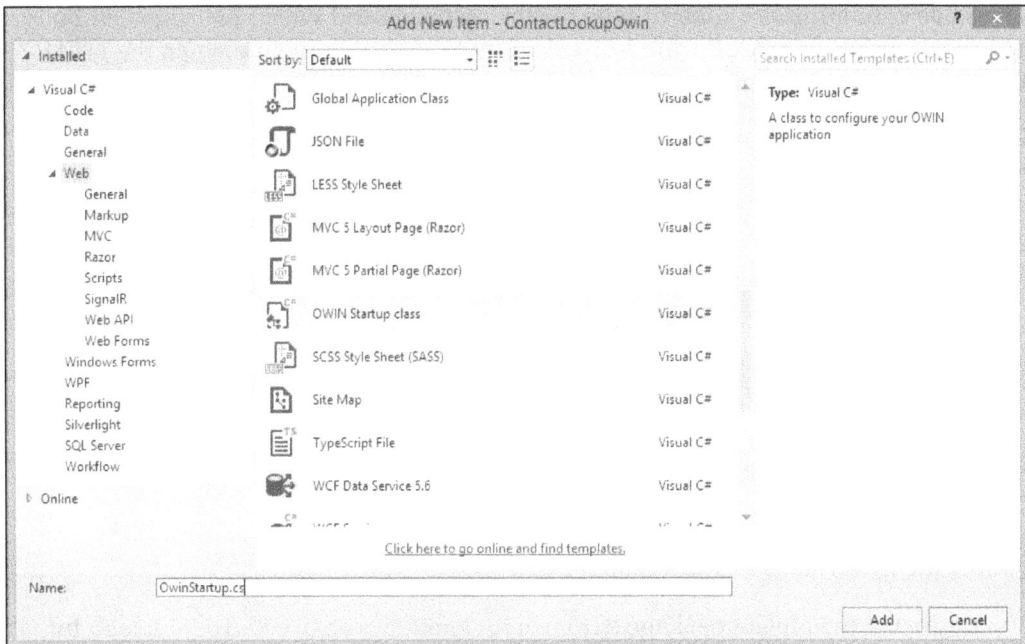

Fig 4 – Added OWIN startup class file named "OwinStartup.cs"

8. Replace the `Configuration` method in the `OwinStartup` class with the following code:

```
public void Configuration(IAppBuilder app)
{
    app.Run(context =>
    {
        context.Response.ContentType = "text/plain";
        return context.Response.WriteAsync("Owin Startup.");
    });
}
```

This code configures the content type for the response and writes the response body. This happens as the middleware is invoked by the OWIN pipeline when the HTTP request is received by the server.

Run the application by pressing *F5* and you will see the following output in a browser:

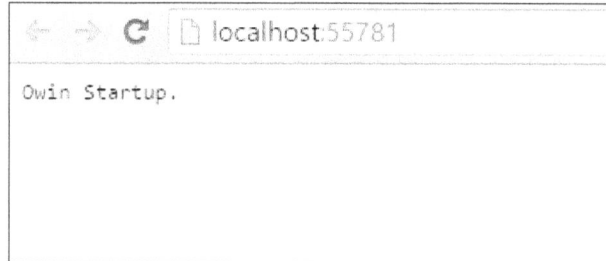

Fig 5 – Response with the injected content "Owin Startup."

Follow the given steps to add Web API to the OWIN pipeline:

1. Install the NuGet package `Microsoft.AspNet.WebApi.OwinSelfHost` by running the following command in the package manager console:

    ```
    Install-Package Microsoft.AspNet.WebApi.OwinSelfHost
    ```

2. This package enables the application to host ASP.NET Web API in our process using the OWIN HttpListener server.

3. Modify the `Configuration` method in `Owin Startup` class as given in the following code:

    ```
    public void Configuration(IAppBuilder app)
    {
            HttpConfiguration config = new HttpConfiguration();
            config.Routes.MapHttpRoute(
                name: "DefaultApi",
                routeTemplate: "api/{controller}/{id}",
                defaults: new { id = RouteParameter.Optional }
            );

            app.UseWebApi(config);

            app.Run(context =>
            {
                context.Response.ContentType = "text/plain";
                return context.Response.WriteAsync("Owin
    Startup.");
            });
    }
    ```

4. Add a new class file named `ContactsController` and inherit from `ApiController` as given in the following:

```
public class ContactsController : ApiController
    {
        Contact[] contacts = new Contact[]
        {
            new Contact { Id = 1, Name = "Steve", Email = "steve@
gmail.com", Mobile = "+1(234)35434" },
            new Contact { Id = 2, Name = "Matt", Email = "matt@
gmail.com", Mobile = "+1(234)5654" },
            new Contact { Id = 3, Name = "Mark", Email = "mark@
gmail.com", Mobile = "+1(234)56789" }
        };


  public async Task<IHttpActionResult> GetAllContacts()
  {
        return Json(contacts);
  }

        public class Contact
        {
            public int Id { get; set; }
            public string Name { get; set; }
            public string Email { get; set; }
            public string Mobile { get; set; }
        }
    }
```

5. Run the application by pressing *F5* and go to `http://localhost:55781/api/contacts` in a browser, as shown in the following screenshot:

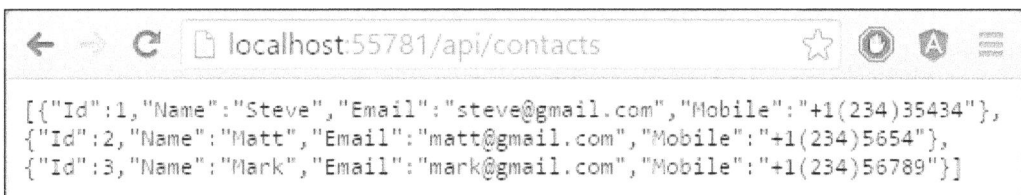

Fig 6 – Contacts Web API controller returns list of contacts in JSON format

6. Notice that we have successfully added Web API to the OWIN pipeline and ran it.

Individual User Account authentication flow

Individual User login in Web API uses OAuth2 to authenticate the requests using the resource owner password flow. Resource owner password flow is a grand type that is defined in OAuth2. This authentication flow enables the client to send username and password to authorization server. The basic flow of a local login is given in the following:

1. The end user provides username and password on client screen.
2. The client sends the username and password to the server that returns an access token.
3. The server verifies the username and password received and returns an access token.
4. The client accesses protected resources by sending the access token along with an HTTP request in the **Authorization** header.

The following image shows the basic flow of the OAuth2 authentication:

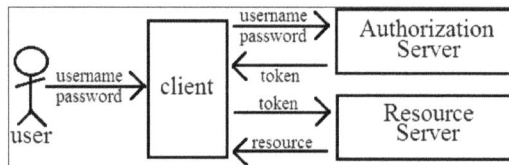

Fig 7 – Resource owner password flow

The following diagram shows the authentication process in ASP.NET Web API. Authorization server in Web API takes care of authenticating the requests and issuing tokens. Here, the Resource servers are Web API controllers. So, to protect Web API controllers from unauthorized access, we need to decorate those controllers with [Authorize] attribute. The requests must be authenticated if the controller or action decorated with [Authorize] attribute. If the request is not authenticated, then Web API will return 401 (Unauthorized) error as the authorization is denied:

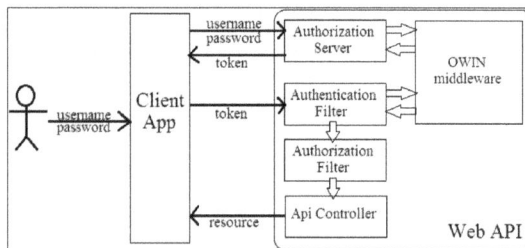

Fig 8 – The Web API authentication flow

Sending an unauthorized request

To view the outcome of sending an unauthorized request to a Web API controller, which is decorated with Authorize attribute, let's create a Web API by following the given steps:

1. Create **New Project** from the **Start** page in Visual Studio.

2. Select **Visual C# Installed Template** named **Web**.

3. Select **ASP.NET Web Application** in the center pane.

4. Name the project WebAPIWithAuthorize and click **OK**:

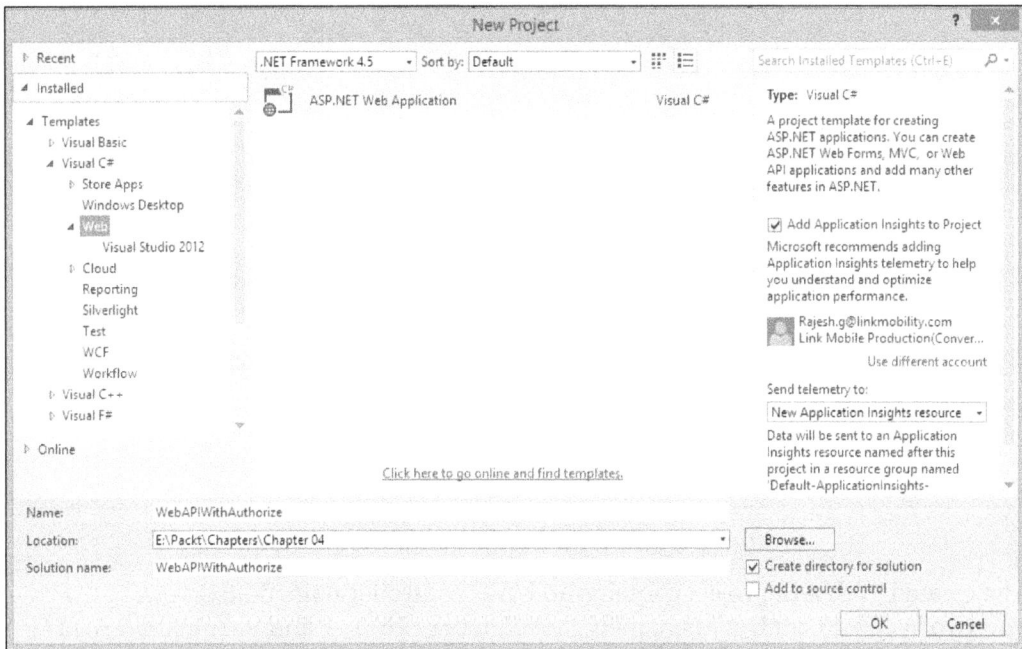

Fig 9 – We have named the ASP.NET Web Application as "WebAPIWithAuthorize"

5. Select the **Web API** template in the **New ASP.NET Project** dialog. This will select **Web API** and **MVC** by default under **Add folders and core references**.

6. Click **OK** to create the application, leaving **Authentication** as **Individual User Accounts** by default:

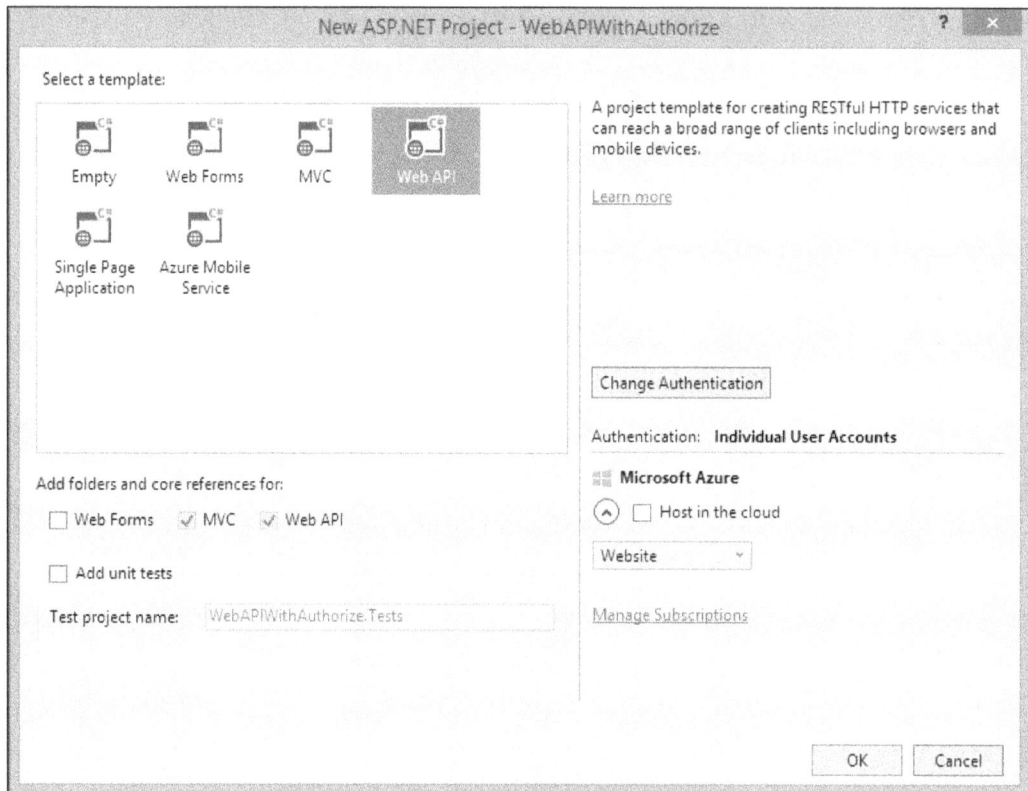

Fig 10 – We have selected Web API

The created Web API project contains an MVC controller named `HomeController` and two Web API controllers namely, `AccountController` and `ValuesController`. `AccountController` deals with user account operations, such as registration, log in, log out, password changes, and so on. `ValuesController` is a Web API controller with some basic operations, such as illustrations. You will notice that this controller is decorated with the `[Authorize]` attribute. So only authenticated requests can access this controller:

```
[Authorize]
public class ValuesController : ApiController
{
    ...
}
```

Let's run the application and browse the URL `http://localhost:61486/api/Values/`. You will get the following authorization error:

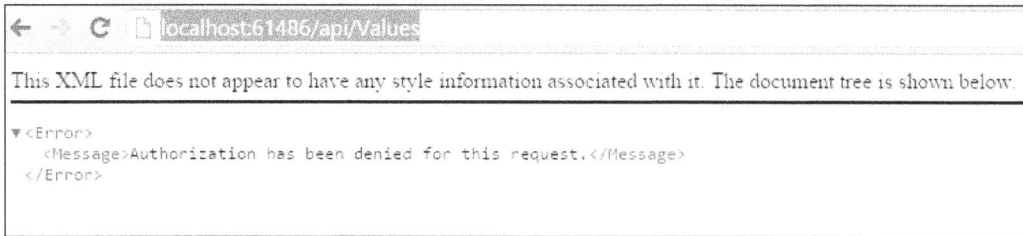

Fig 11 – Unauthorized access error occurred

I also captured the request and response for this operation using Fiddler for you, as follows:

`GET http://localhost:61486/api/Values HTTP/1.1`

`Host: localhost:61486`

The response that I received is given in the following:

`HTTP/1.1 401 Unauthorized`

`Cache-Control: no-cache`

`Pragma: no-cache`

`Content-Type: application/json; charset=utf-8`

`Expires: -1`

`Server: Microsoft-IIS/8.0`

`X-AspNet-Version: 4.0.30319`

`WWW-Authenticate: Bearer`

`X-Powered-By: ASP.NET`

`Date: Sun, 09 Aug 2015 09:14:21 GMT`

`Content-Length: 61`

`{"Message":"Authorization has been denied for this request."}`

As you can see in the message that was received in response body, the request has been denied as it was not authenticated and the response returned 401 HTTP status code. This happens because the Authorization header is missing in the request since there is no bearer token.

Get an access token

To send an authenticated request to `ValuesController`, we need to pass an access token in the Authorization header. How do we get this access token? To get this access token, we need to log in the application.

Let's first register a user by posting an instance of the user to the Web API Register action method in the Account controller, as follows:

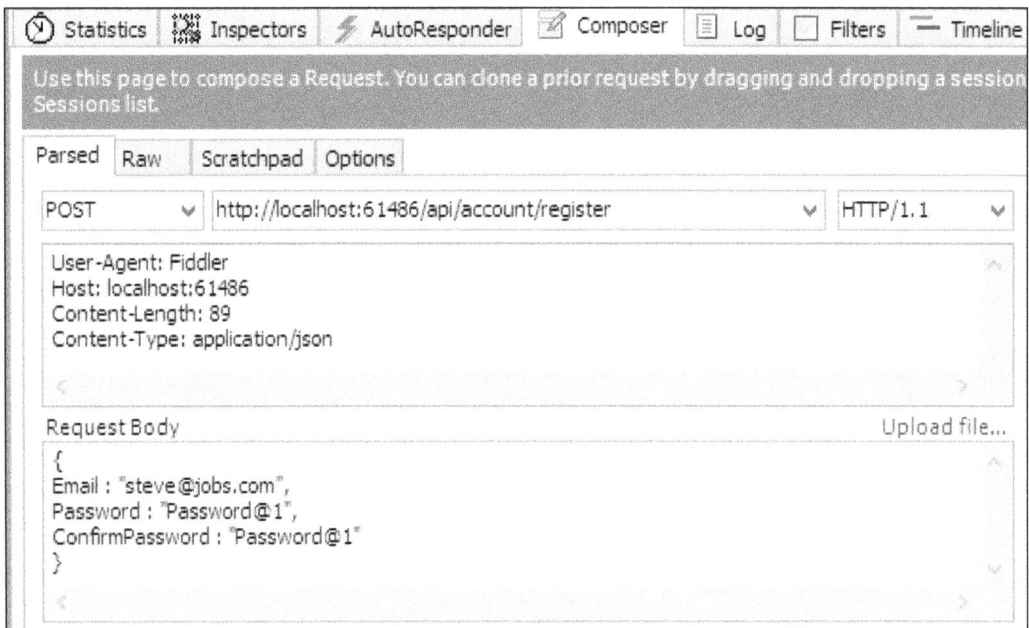

Fig 12 – POSTing an instance of User to Web API

Now, we have a registered user with the username `steve@jobs.com` and password `Password@1`. Let's send form with URL encoded data in the request body to the token endpoint, as follows:

```
{
    "grant_type": "password",
    "username": "steve@jobs.com",
    "Password": "Password@1"
}
```

Let's send this instance to the `Token` endpoint using Fiddler as given in the following:

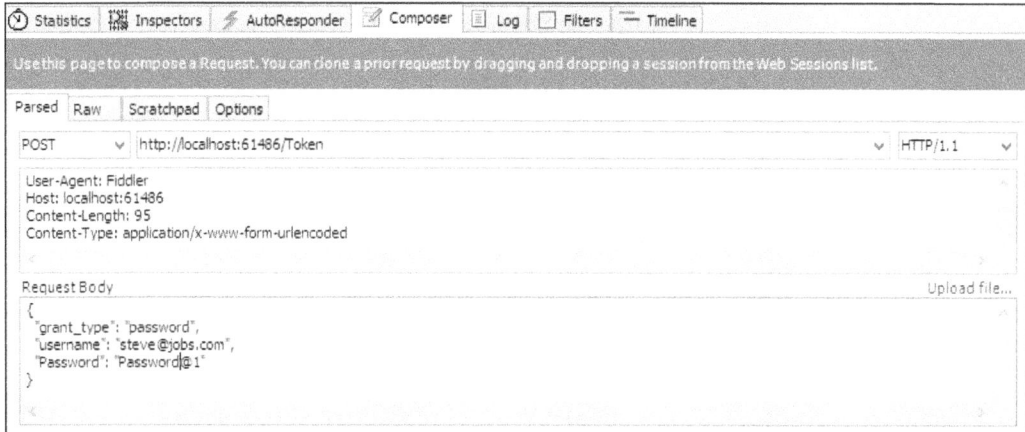

Fig 13 – POSTing an instance of User with the grant type to Token endpoint

We will receive a response with the token in the Set-Cookie header, as shown in the following screenshot:

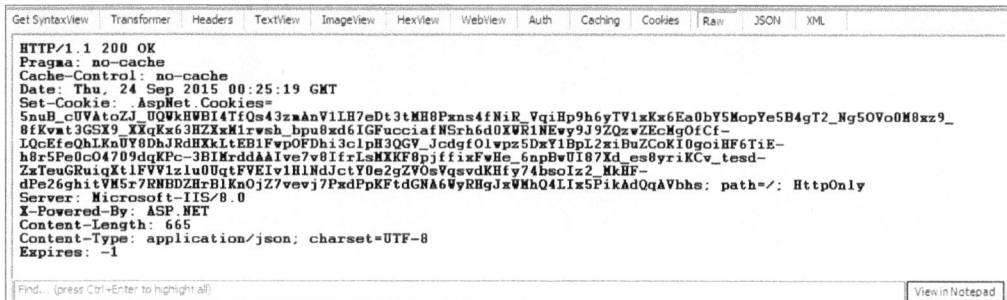

Fig 14 – Response with Token in the Set Cookie header

You can also send this data using the AJAX post request or C#. To demonstrate how to get the token using C#, we introduced an action named `GetToken` in `HomeController` and a view for the same. The C# code for `GetToken` is as follows:

```
public ActionResult GetToken()
{
    var body = new List<KeyValuePair<string, string>>
    {
        new KeyValuePair<string, string>( "grant_type", "password" ),
        new KeyValuePair<string, string>( "username", "test@test.com"
    ),
        new KeyValuePair<string, string> ( "Password", "Sample@1" )
    };
```

```
    var content = new FormUrlEncodedContent(body);

    using (var client = new HttpClient())
    {
        var response = client.PostAsync("http://localhost:61486/
Token", content).Result;
        var result = response.Content.ReadAsStringAsync().Result;

        ViewBag.token = JsonConvert.DeserializeObject<Dictionary<stri
ng, string>>(result)["access_token"];
    }
    return View();
}
```

We construct the body of request with the username and password along with grant type. Then, we post the content to the URL `http://localhost:61486/Token/`. Finally, we deserialize the response content and assign the access token to the ViewBag named token. In the `GetToken` view, we print the access token assigned to view bag, as given in the following screenshot:

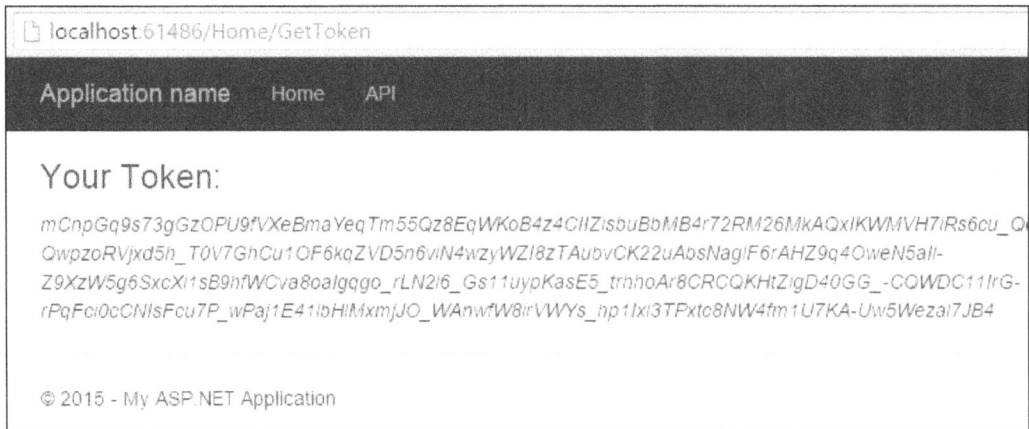

Fig 15 – The retrieved access token printed on the view

Send an authenticated request

In the previous section, we achieved how to retrieve the access token from the server by passing `username` and `password`. Now, with the help of the access token that is received, let's send the authenticated request. The authenticated request will have an Authorization header in the request. We send the request via Fiddler. The request and response is given in the following screenshot:

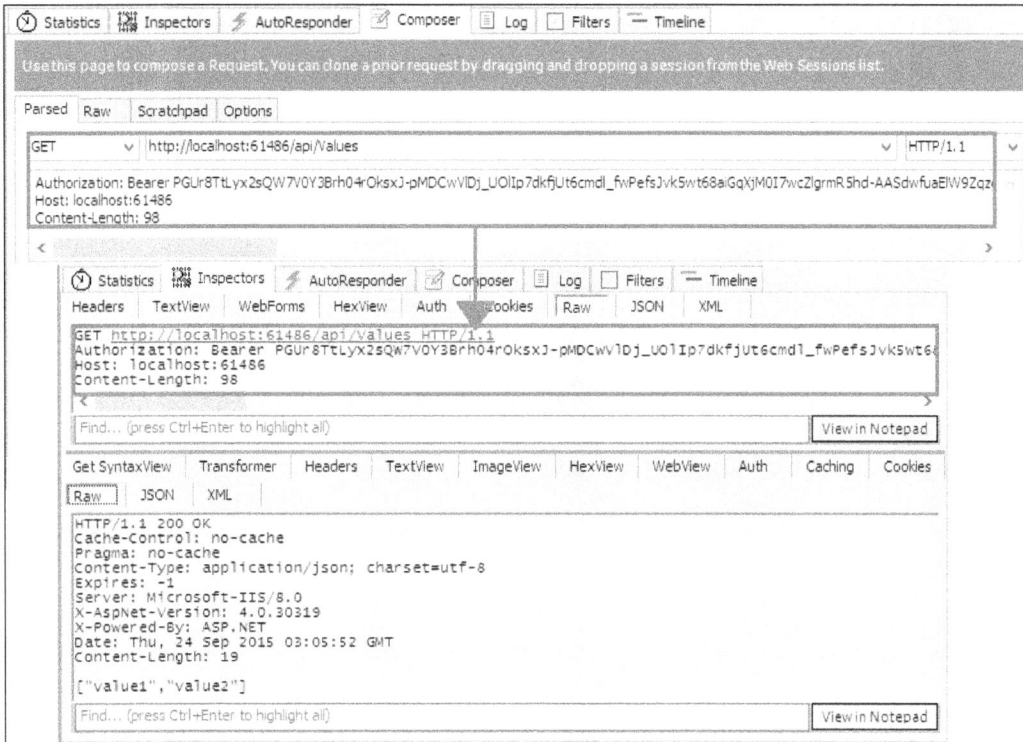

Fig 16 – Sending Authorized request with bearer token

We can also send a `Bearer` token in the header using `HttpClient` in C# code, as follows:

```
using (var client = new HttpClient())
{
        var token = "access_token";
        client.DefaultRequestHeaders.Add("Authorization", String.
Concat("Bearer ", token));
        var response = client.GetAsync("http://localhost:61486/api/
Values").Result;
        var values = response.Content.ReadAsStringAsync().Result;
}
```

> Note: It is always advisable to set up SSL for Web API that facilitates this type of authentication mechanism.

Summary

Hurray! We just secured our Web API using the token-based authentication.

In this chapter, you learned about hosting OWIN in IIS and adding Web API to the OWIN pipeline. You also learned and understood the flow of Local Login Authentication.

We did a walkthrough of how to send an unauthorized request and understood its impact.

Then, we sent the username and password to get an access token for further access of the resources that require an authenticated request.

Finally, you saw how to send the bearer token in the Authorization header of the request and access the protected resources.

In the next chapter, let's secure Web API by enabling the basic authentication using authentication filters.

Let's step up our security to the next level!

5

Enabling Basic Authentication using Authentication Filter in Web API

This chapter will show how to set an authentication scheme for individual controllers or actions using an Authentication filter that implements the HTTP Basic Authentication scheme and also discuss the advantages and disadvantages of using Basic Authentication.

In this chapter, we will learn the following topics:

- Basic authentication with IIS
- Basic authentication with custom membership
- Basic authentication using an authentication filter
- Setting an authentication filter
- Implementing a Web API authentication filter
- Setting an error result
- Combining authentication filters with host-level authentication

Basic authentication with IIS

Internet Information Services(IIS) enables authenticating the user based on their Windows credentials. So it is necessary that the user must have a domain server account. Basic authentication in IIS is built to authenticate using the Windows credentials.

The following steps will enable basic authentication using IIS:

1. Open your **ASP.NET Application** from the **Start** page in Visual Studio.

2. Open the **Web.config** file.

3. Set authentication mode to **Windows** in the **Web.config** file:

```
<system.web>
    <authentication mode="Windows" />
</system.web>
```

4. Open **IIS Manager**.

5. Go to **Features View**.

6. Select **Authentication** in **IIS Manger**:

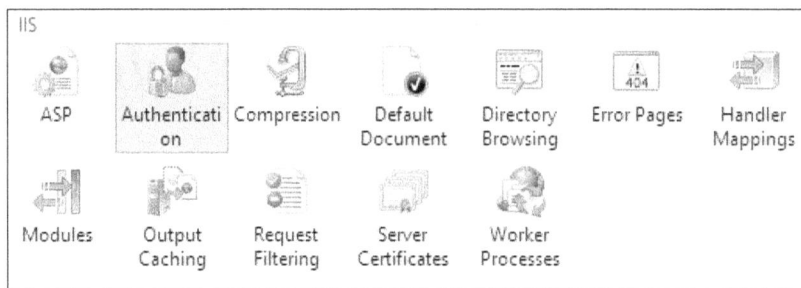

Fig 1 – Select authentication in features view

7. Disable **Anonymous Authentication** and enable **Basic Authentication**:

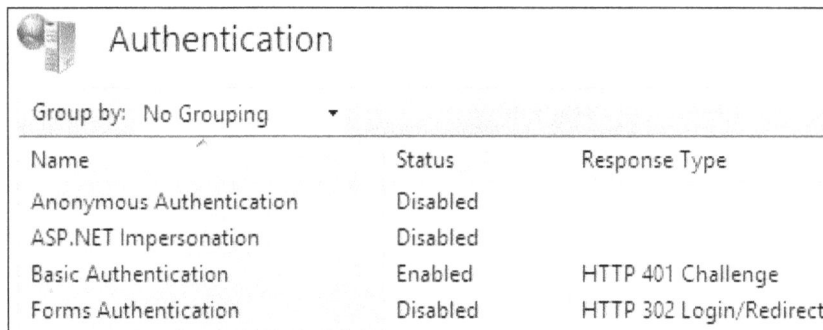

Fig 2 – Right-click and enable basic authentication

> If you don't find **Basic Authentication** under **Authentication**, go to **Programs and Features**, turn on or off **Windows Components**, and enable **Basic Authentication** under **IIS | World Wide Web Services | Security**.

Basic authentication with custom membership

We just saw how to enable basic authentication with IIS. However, if the website is a publically available website, it is not possible to authenticate the user using Windows credentials. In such cases, the website should authenticate using the ASP.NET membership provider. In order to achieve this, we need to implement a custom membership with basic authentication.

Custom membership with basic authentication can be implemented using an HTTP module as given in the following:

```
public class BasicAuthHttpModule : IHttpModule
{
    //...
}
```

We need to create two methods and hook them to the `AuthenticateRequest` and `EndRequest` events in the `Init` method as given in the following code:

```
public void Init(HttpApplication context)
{
    context.AuthenticateRequest +=
                        OnApplicationAuthenticateRequest;
    context.EndRequest += OnApplicationEndRequest;
}
```

As you can see `OnApplicationAuthenticateRequest` is added or registered to the `AuthenticateRequest` event of `HttpApplication` and `OnApplicationEndRequest` is added or registered to the `EndRequest` event of `HttpApplication`.

The `OnApplicationAuthenticateRequest` method should check the `Authorization` request in the request header as follows:

```
var request = HttpContext.Current.Request;
var authHeader = request.Headers["Authorization"];
if (authHeader != null)
{
    //...
}
```

If the `Authorization` header contains information for Basic Authentication, then the username and password should be extracted from the credentials and validated using the ASP.NET membership provider that is injected into the HTTP module, as follows:

```
var encoding = Encoding.GetEncoding("iso-8859-1");
var credentials = encoding.GetString(Convert.
FromBase64String(authHeader.Parameter));
int separator = credentials.IndexOf(':');
string name = credentials.Substring(0, separator);
string password = credentials.Substring(separator + 1);
```

If the obtained username and password are valid, then it creates IPrincipal and assigns it to the current user of the HTTP context as shown in the following code:

```
// If credential is valid, then build the principal
var identity = new GenericIdentity(name);
Thread.CurrentPrincipal = new GenericPrincipal(identity, null));
if (HttpContext.Current != null)
{
    HttpContext.Current.User = principal;
}
```

Add the following code in the `web.config` file under the `system.webServer` section to enable the HTTP module:

```
<modules>
        <add name="BasicAuthHttpModule"
          type="ContactLookup.Modules.BasicAuthHttpModule,
AssemblyName"/>
</modules>
```

Replace `AssemblyName` with the actual name of the assembly, excluding the `dll` extension. Also, we need to disable other authentications, such as **Form** and Windows authentication.

Basic authentication using an authentication filter

With the release of ASP.NET Web API 2.0, it is best practice to use an authentication filter for basic authentication rather than using an HTTP module. Follow the given steps to implement basic authentication using an authentication filter:

1. Create **New Project** from the **Start** page in Visual Studio.
2. Select **Visual C# Installed Template** named **Web**.
3. Select **ASP.NET Web Application** in the center pane.
4. Name the project Chapter05.BasicAuthentication and click **OK**:

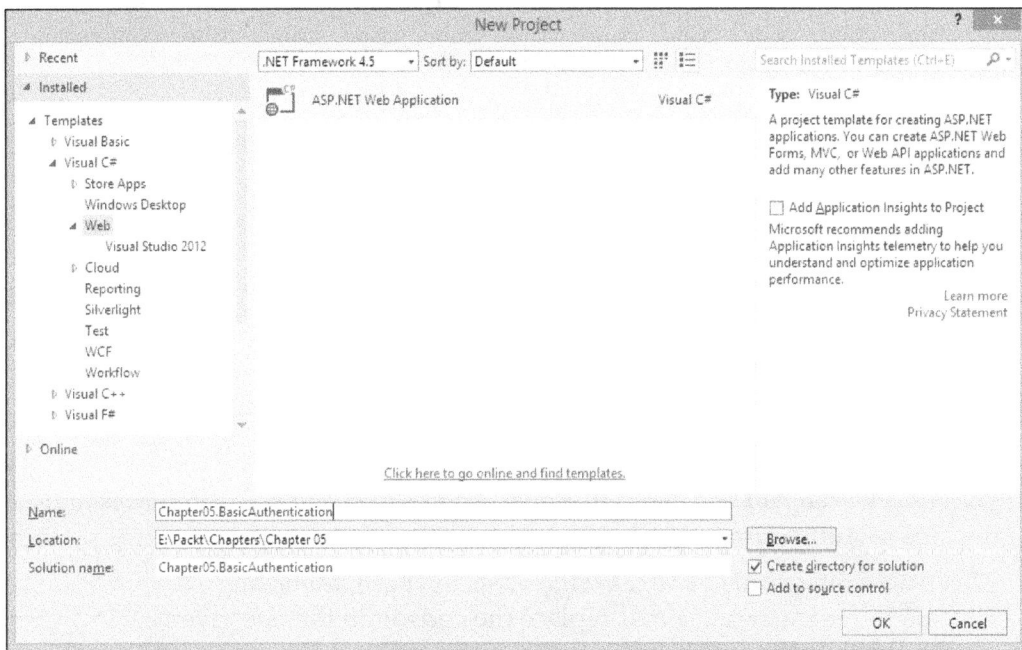

Fig 3 – We have named the ASP.NET Web Application as "Chapter05.BasicAuthentication"

5. Select the **MVC** template in the **New ASP.NET Project** dialog.

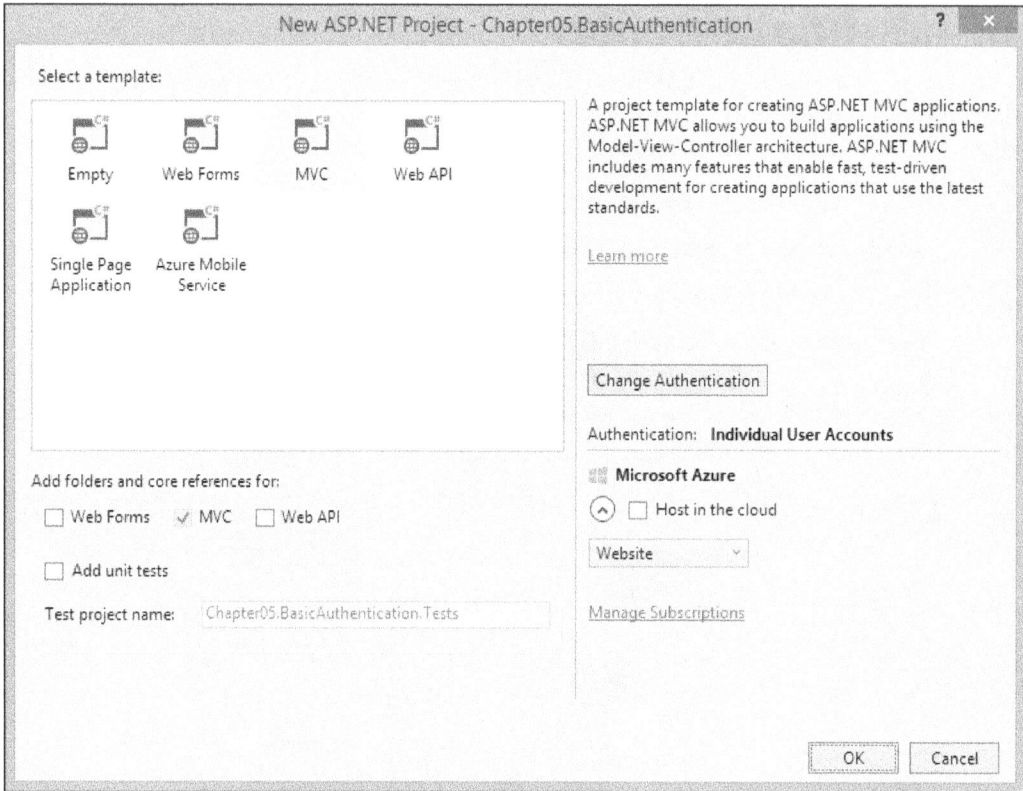

Fig 4 – Select MVC template and check Web API in add folders and core references

6. Check **Web API** and click **OK** under **Add folders and core references** and leave **Authentication** to **Individual User Accounts**:

7. Add a filter named `BasicAuthorizeAttribute`, inheriting `AuthorizeAttribute` and replace the code with the one given in the following:

```
namespace Chapter05.BasicAuthentication.Filters
{
    public class BasicAuthorizeAttribute : System.Web.Http.
AuthorizeAttribute
    {
        private const string BasicAuthResponseHeader = "WWW-
Authenticate";
        private const string BasicAuthResponseHeaderValue =
"Basic";
```

```
        public override void OnAuthorization(HttpActionContext
actionContext)
        {
            try
            {
                var authValue = actionContext.Request.Headers.
Authorization;

                if (authValue != null && !String.
IsNullOrWhiteSpace(authValue.Parameter) && authValue.Scheme ==
BasicAuthResponseHeaderValue)
                {
                    var credentials = ParseAuthorizationHeader(aut
hValue.Parameter);

                    if (credentials != null)
                    {
                        // Check if the username and passowrd in
credentials are valid against the ASP.NET membership.
                        // If valid, the set the current principal
in the request context
                        var identity = new
GenericIdentity(credentials.Username);
                        actionContext.RequestContext.Principal =
new GenericPrincipal(identity, null);
                    }
                }
                else
                {
                    actionContext.Response =
GetUnauthorizedResponse();
                    return;
                }
            }
            catch (Exception)
            {
                actionContext.Response =
GetUnauthorizedResponse();
                return;

            }
        }

        private Credentials ParseAuthorizationHeader(string
authHeader)
        {
            var credentials = Encoding.ASCII.GetString(Convert.
FromBase64String(authHeader)).Split(new[] { ':' });
```

```
                if (credentials.Length != 2 || string.
IsNullOrEmpty(credentials[0]) || string.
IsNullOrEmpty(credentials[1]))
                    return null;

                return new Credentials() { Username = credentials[0],
Password = credentials[1], };
            }

            private HttpResponseMessage GetUnauthorizedResponse()
            {
                var response = new HttpResponseMessage(HttpStatusCode.
Unauthorized);
                response.Headers.Add(BasicAuthResponseHeader,
BasicAuthResponseHeaderValue);
                return response;
            }
        }
        public class Credentials
        {
            public string Username { get; set; }
            public string Password { get; set; }
        }
    }
```

8. As you can see in the code, the `OnAuthorization` method checks the `Authorization` in request header. If the `Authroization` header is available along with the basic authentication information, then it tries to extract the username and password from the `Base64` encoded token value. The user credentials that are extracted will be validated against the ASP.NET membership for authentication.

9. Add a Web API controller named `ContactsController` and replace the code with the following code:

```
namespace Chapter05.BasicAuthentication.Api
{
    public class ContactsController : ApiController
    {
        IEnumerable<Contact> contacts = new List<Contact>
        {
            new Contact { Id = 1, Name = "Steve", Email = "steve@
gmail.com", Mobile = "+1(234)35434" },
            new Contact { Id = 2, Name = "Matt", Email = "matt@
gmail.com", Mobile = "+1(234)5654" },
            new Contact { Id = 3, Name = "Mark", Email = "mark@
gmail.com", Mobile = "+1(234)56789" }
```

```
        };

        [BasicAuthorize]
        // GET: api/Contacts
        public IEnumerable<Contact> Get()
        {
            return contacts;
        }
    }
}
```

The `BasicAuthorize` attribute can also be configured at controller or application level. This can be achieved by decorating the controller with this attribute or configuring it in a `global.asax` file to enable it in application.

10. The `Get` action in `ContactsController` is decorated with the `BasicAuthorize` attribute, which is a custom attribute that we created for basic authentication. So only a request with valid basic authentication details in the header can access the `GET` action in the API controller.

Setting an authentication filter

The `http://aspnet.codeplex.com` provides the sample code for the authentication filter named `IdentityBasicAuthenticationAttribute` that implements HTTP Basic Access Authentication scheme (RFC 2617). We can make use of this `[IdentityBasicAuthentication]` authentication filter and apply it at the action level, controller level, or global level that can be applied to all the controllers and actions.

Action-level authentication filter

To apply a basic authentication filter at action level, we need to decorate the respective actions with the `[IdentityBasicAuthentication]` filter as given in the following:

```
// Require authenticated requests.
public class ContactsController : ApiController
{
    public HttpResponseMessage GetContact() { . . . }

    // Enable Basic authentication for this action
    [IdentityBasicAuthentication]
    public HttpResponseMessage PostContact(Contact contact) { . . . }
}
```

Controller-level authentication filter

If we decorate the basic authentication filter at controller level, then accessing all the actions inside that controller need an authenticated request. Applying the basic authentication filter at controller level is given in the following:

```
// Enable Basic authentication for this controller
[IdentityBasicAuthentication]
// Require authenticated requests.
[Authorize]
public class ContactsController : ApiController
{
    public HttpResponseMessage GetContact() { . . . }
    public HttpResponseMessage PostContact(Contact contact) { . . . }
}
```

Global-level authentication filter

We can apply any filter globally in Web API by adding the filter to the collection of filters in the `webApiConfig` class file as given in the following. This code adds the `IdentityBasicAuthentication` filter to the collection of filters, as follows:

```
public static class WebApiConfig
{
    public static void Register(HttpConfiguration config)
    {
        config.Filters.Add(new
IdentityBasicAuthenticationAttribute());
        //...
    }
}
```

Implementing a Web API authentication filter

An authentication filter in Web API must implement the `System.Web.Http.Filters.IAuthenticationFilter` interface. The interface contains a `AllowMultiple` property of Boolean type that indicates that more than one instance of the attribute can be specified for a single program element. It has two methods, namely `AuthenticateAsync` to validate credentials in the request and `ChallengeAsync` to attach an authentication challenge to the response, if required.

As the filter can be decorated to the controllers and actions, we also need to inherit from `System.Attribute`.

Before executing an action in a Web API controller, it first builds a list of authentication filters that are configured globally, at controller level and that particular action level. Then it calls the `AuthenticateAsync` method in each filter that is found in the list. The `AuthenticateAsync` method in each filter validates the credentials in the request and if any succeed with credential validation, then it creates IPrincipal and attaches it to the request. Code snippet of the `AuthenticateAsync` method from Basic Authentication sample in CodePlex is given in the following:

```
public async Task AuthenticateAsync(HttpAuthenticationContext context,
CancellationToken cancellationToken)
{
    // 1. Look for credentials in the request.
    HttpRequestMessage request = context.Request;
    AuthenticationHeaderValue authorization = request.Headers.
Authorization;

    // 2. If there are no credentials, do nothing.
    if (authorization == null)
    {
        return;
    }

    // 3. If there are credentials but the filter does not recognize
the
    //    authentication scheme, do nothing.
    if (authorization.Scheme != "Basic")
    {
        return;
    }

    // 4. If there are credentials that the filter understands, try to
validate them.
    // 5. If the credentials are bad, set the error result.
    if (String.IsNullOrEmpty(authorization.Parameter))
    {
        context.ErrorResult = new AuthenticationFailureResult("Missing
credentials", request);
        return;
    }

    Tuple<string, string> userNameAndPasword = ExtractUserNameAndPassw
ord(authorization.Parameter);
```

```
    if (userNameAndPasword == null)
    {
        context.ErrorResult = new AuthenticationFailureResult("Invalid
credentials", request);
    }

    string userName = userNameAndPasword.Item1;
    string password = userNameAndPasword.Item2;

    IPrincipal principal = await AuthenticateAsync(userName, password,
cancellationToken);
    if (principal == null)
    {
        context.ErrorResult = new AuthenticationFailureResult("Invalid
username or password", request);
    }

    // 6. If the credentials are valid, set principal.
    else
    {
        context.Principal = principal;
    }

}
```

Once IPrincipal is successfully created, Web API executes the `ChallengeAsync` method in available filters in the list to add challenge to the response. Code snippet of the `ChallengeAsync` method is shown in the following:

```
public Task ChallengeAsync(HttpAuthenticationChallengeContext context,
CancellationToken cancellationToken)
{
    var challenge = new AuthenticationHeaderValue("Basic");
    context.Result = new AddChallengeOnUnauthorizedResult(challenge,
context.Result);
    return Task.FromResult(0);
}
```

Setting an error result

If the credentials are found to be invalid by any of the filters in the list, then it sets
`ErrorResult` in context parameter of the `AuthenticateAsync` method. Instance
of `AuthenticationFailureResult` is assigned to context with appropriate error
message as follows in the `AuthenticateAsync` method of the filter:

```
    // If the sufficient information for credentials not supplied.
    if (String.IsNullOrEmpty(authorization.Parameter))
    {
        context.ErrorResult = new AuthenticationFailureResult("Missing
credentials", request);
        return;
    }

    Tuple<string, string> userNameAndPasword = ExtractUserNameAndPassw
ord(authorization.Parameter);
    string userName = userNameAndPasword.Item1;
    string password = userNameAndPasword.Item2;

    IPrincipal principal = await AuthenticateAsync(userName, password,
cancellationToken);

    // if the provided username and password is not valid
    if (principal == null)
    {
        context.ErrorResult = new AuthenticationFailureResult("Invalid
username or password", request);
    }
```

Combining authentication filters with host-level authentication

Authentication at host level will be carried out by the host, such as IIS, itself even
before the request reaches the Web API framework. We can disable the host-level
authentication in Web API by calling the `config.SuppressHostPrincipal()`
method in the Web API configuration as given in the following:

```
public static class WebApiConfig
{
    public static void Register(HttpConfiguration config)
    {
        config.SuppressHostPrincipal();
    }
}
```

It is best practice to disable the host-level authentication in Web API and enable it for the rest of the application. Once the host-level authentication is disabled, we can apply the authentication filter that was created in the earlier section at application level, controller level, or action level for Web API.

Summary

Bravo! We just secured our Web API using basic authentication.

You learned how to configure basic authentication in IIS and implemented basic authentication using custom membership.

We have seen how to set an authentication filter at different levels and did a step-by-step walkthrough of how to implement Authentication Filter in ASP.NET Web API.

You also learned how to set the error result if authentication failed.

Finally, we saw how to suppress host-level authentication in ASP.NET Web API.

In the next chapter, let's secure a Web API using Forms and Windows authentication.

6
Securing a Web API using Forms and Windows Authentication

This chapter will cover how to secure Web API using Forms and Windows authentication. You will also learn about the advantages and disadvantages of using Forms and Windows authentication in Web API.

In this chapter, we will cover the following topics:

- Working of Forms authentication
- Implementing Forms authentication in Web API
- Discussing Integrated Windows Authentication
- Discussing the advantages and disadvantages of using the Integrated Windows Authentication mechanism
- Configuring Windows authentication
- Discussing the difference between Basic authentication and Windows authentication
- Enabling Windows authentication in Katana

Working of Forms authentication

The user credentials will be submitted to the server using HTML forms in Forms authentication. This can be used in ASP.NET Web API only if it is consumed from web application. Forms authentication is built under ASP.NET and uses the ASP.NET membership provider to manage user accounts. Forms authentication requires browser client to pass the user credentials to the server. It sends the user credentials in the request and uses HTTP cookies for authentication.

Let's list the step-by-step process of Forms authentication, as follows:

1. Browser tries to access a restricted action that requires an authenticated request.

2. If the browser sends an unauthenticated request, then the server will respond with HTTP status 302 Found and triggers the URL redirection to login page.

3. To send the authenticated request, a user enters the username and password, and submits the form.

4. If the credentials are valid, the server responds with HTTP 302 status code that initiates the browser to redirect the page to original requested URL with the authentication cookie in the response.

5. Now, any request from the browser includes the authentication cookie and the server will grant access to any restricted resource.

Implementing Forms authentication in Web API

To send the credentials to the server, we need an HTML form to submit. Let's use the HTML form or HTML view in the ASP.NET MVC application.

Steps to implement Forms authentication in an ASP.NET MVC application are as follows:

1. Create **New Project** from the **Start** page in Visual Studio.

2. Select **Visual C# Installed Template** named **Web**.

3. Choose **ASP.NET Web Application** in the center panel.

4. Name the project as `Chapter06.FormsAuthentication` and click **OK**:

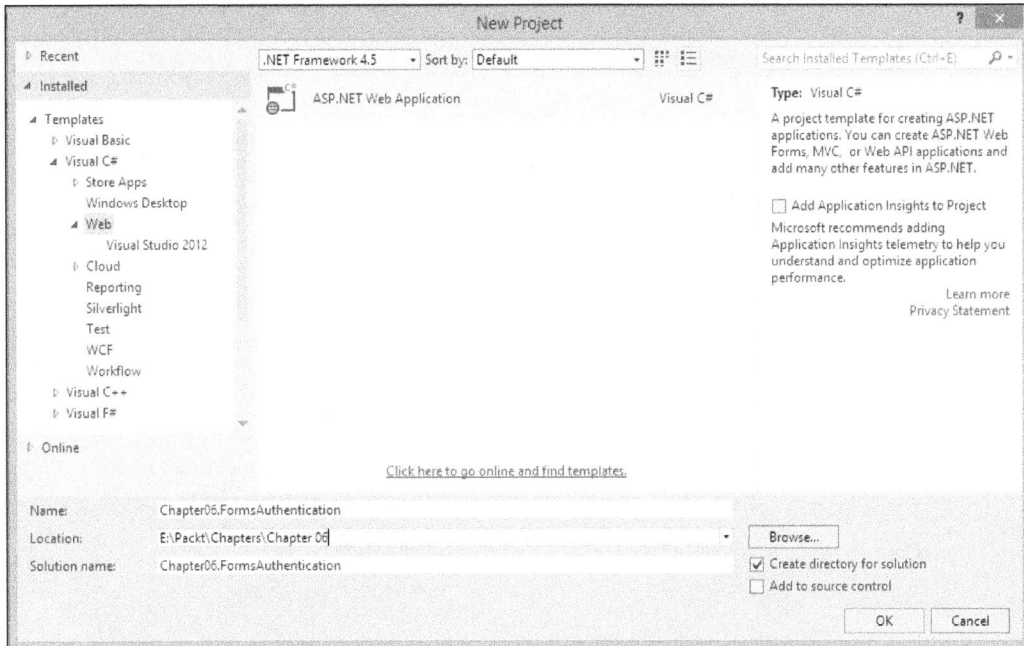

Fig 1 – We have named the ASP.NET Web Application "Chapter06.FormsAuthentication"

5. Select the **MVC** template in the **New ASP.NET Project** dialog.

6. Tick **Web API** under **Add folders and core references** and press **OK**, leaving the **Authentication** to **Individual User Accounts**:

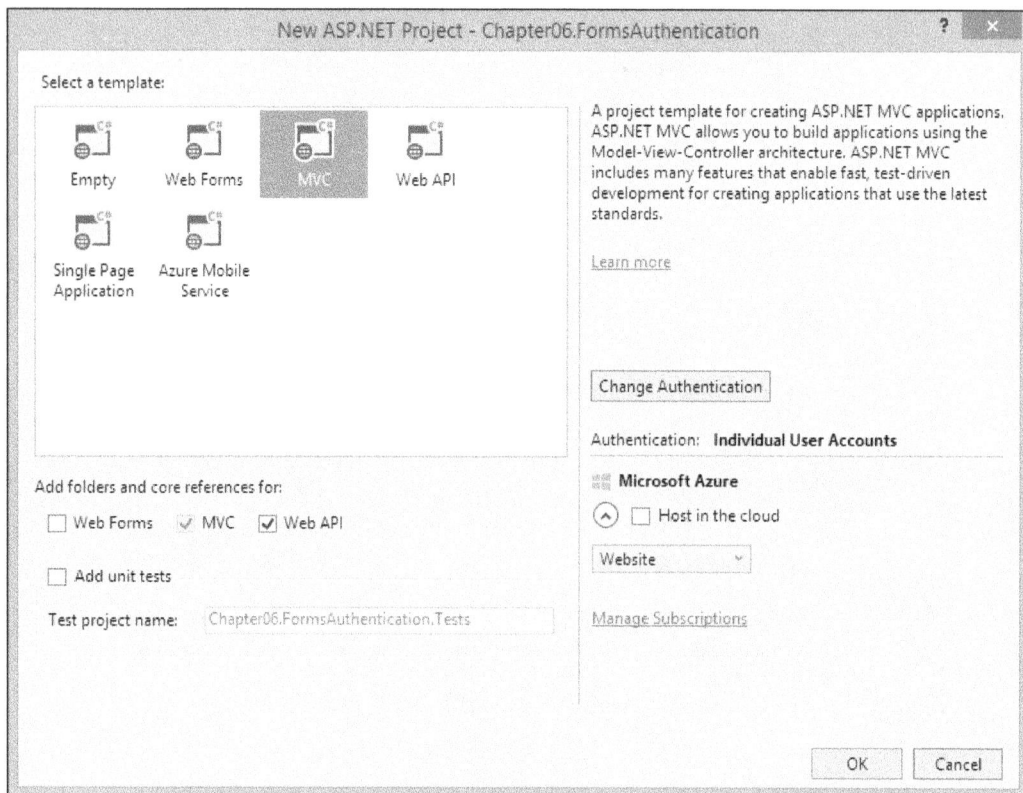

Fig 2 – Select MVC template and check Web API in add folders and core references

7. Forms authentication configuration can be included in the `web.config` file, as follows:

```
<system.web>
    <authentication mode="Forms">
        <forms loginUrl="~/Account/LogOn" timeout="30" />
    </authentication>
</system.web>
```

In this configuration, we set the authentication mode to `"Forms"` and also configured `loginurl` so that the application redirects to the configured page to log in if the request is not authenticated.

8. In the **Models** folder, add a class named `Contact.cs` with the following code:

```
namespace Chapter06.FormsAuthentication.Models
{
    public class Contact
    {
        public int Id { get; set; }
        public string Name { get; set; }
        public string Email { get; set; }
        public string Mobile { get; set; }
    }
}
```

9. Add a Web API controller named `ContactsController` with the following code snippet:

```
namespace Chapter06.FormsAuthentication.Api
{
    public class ContactsController : ApiController
    {
        IEnumerable<Contact> contacts = new List<Contact>
        {
            new Contact { Id = 1, Name = "Steve", Email = "steve@
gmail.com", Mobile = "+1(234)35434" },
            new Contact { Id = 2, Name = "Matt", Email = "matt@
gmail.com", Mobile = "+1(234)5654" },
            new Contact { Id = 3, Name = "Mark", Email = "mark@
gmail.com", Mobile = "+1(234)56789" }
        };

        [Authorize]
        // GET: api/Contacts
        public IEnumerable<Contact> Get()
        {
            return contacts;
        }
    }
}
```

As you can see in the preceding code, we have decorated the `Get()` action in `ContactsController` with the `[Authorize]` attribute. So this Web API action can only be accessed by an authenticated request. An unauthenticated request for this action will make the browser redirect to the login page and enable the user to either register or log in:

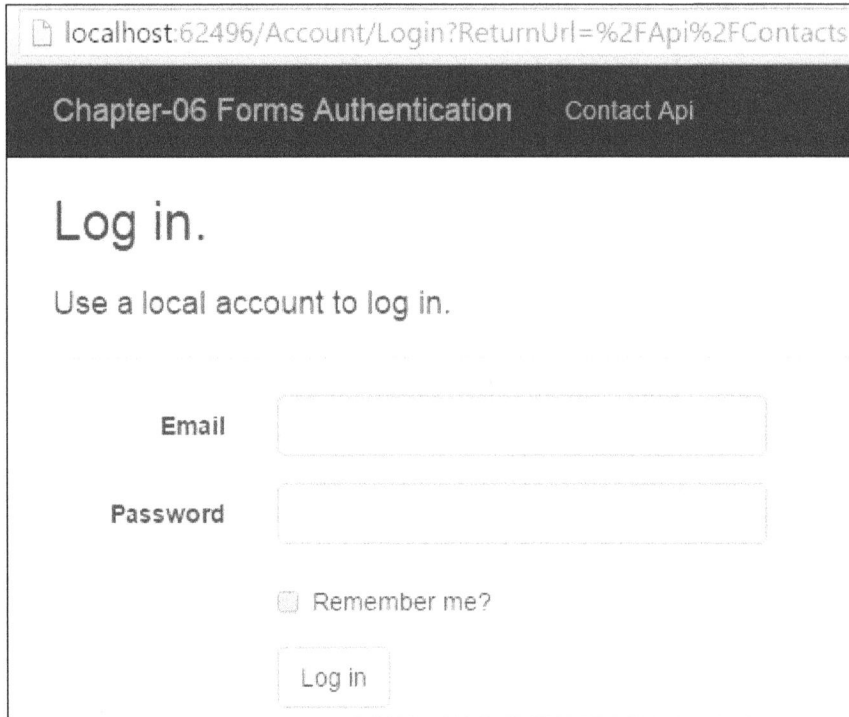

Fig 3 – Redirected Login Page for Authentication

Once logged in, any request that tries to access this action will be allowed as it is authenticated. This is because the browser automatically sends the session cookie along with the request and Forms authentication uses this cookie to authenticate the request:

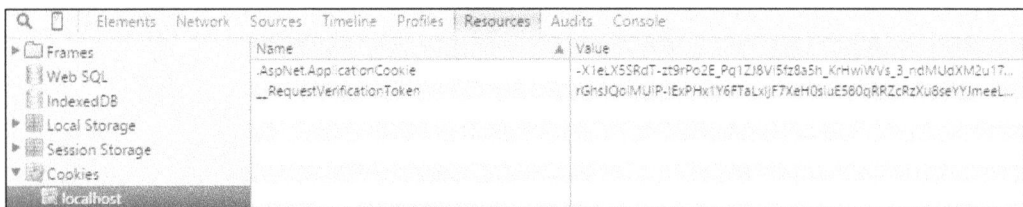

Fig 4 – Authentication Cookie shown in developer tool

> It is very important to secure the website using SSL as Forms authentication sends unencrypted credentials. Refer to *Chapter 2, Enabling SSL for ASP.NET Web API*, to learn how to set up SSL for your application.

What is Integrated Windows Authentication?

Integrated Windows Authentication is an authentication mechanism that is based on SPNEGO, Kerberos, and NTLMSSP protocols. It deals with automatically authenticating the connection between IIS, IE, and active directory.

Advantages and disadvantages of using the Integrated Windows Authentication mechanism

First let's see the advantages of Windows authentication. Windows authentication is built in IIS. It doesn't send the user credentials along with the request. This authentication mechanism is best suited for intranet applications.

However, with all these advantages, there are few disadvantages on Windows authentication mechanism. It requires Kerberos, which works based on tickets or NTLM, a Microsoft security protocol that should be supported by client. Client PC must be under an active directory domain.

Configuring Windows Authentication

Let's implement Windows authentication to an ASP.NET MVC application following the given steps:

1. Create **New Project** from the **Start** page in Visual Studio.
2. Select **Visual C# Installed Template** named Web.
3. Choose **ASP.NET Web Application** in the center panel.

4.   Name the project `Chapter06.WindowsAuthentication` and click **OK**:

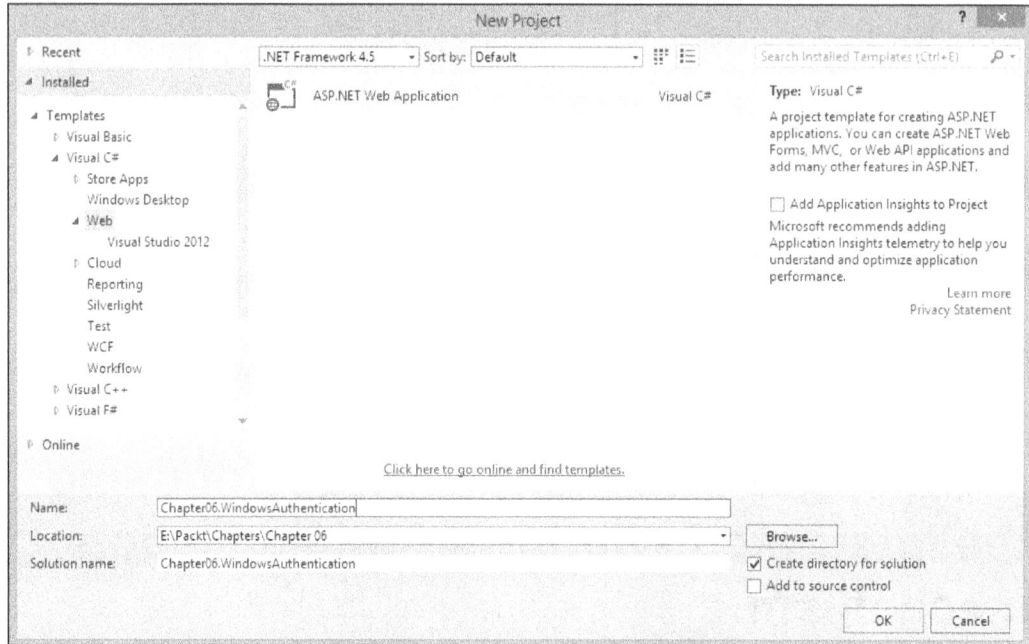

Fig 5 – We have named the ASP.NET Web Application "Chapter06.WindowsAuthentication"

5.   Change the **Authentication** mode to **Windows Authentication**:

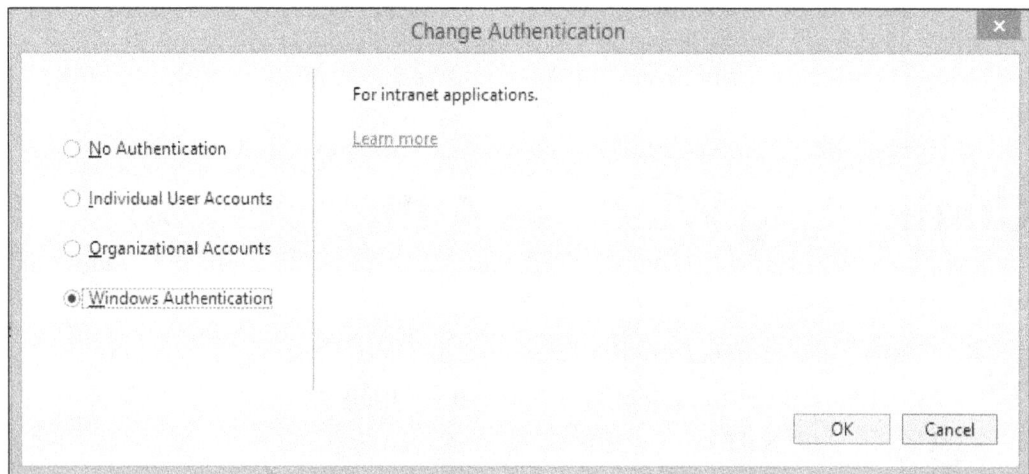

Fig 6 – Select Windows Authentication in Change Authentication window

6.   Select the **MVC** template in the **New ASP.NET Project** dialog.

7. Tick **Web API** under **Add folders and core references** and click **OK**:

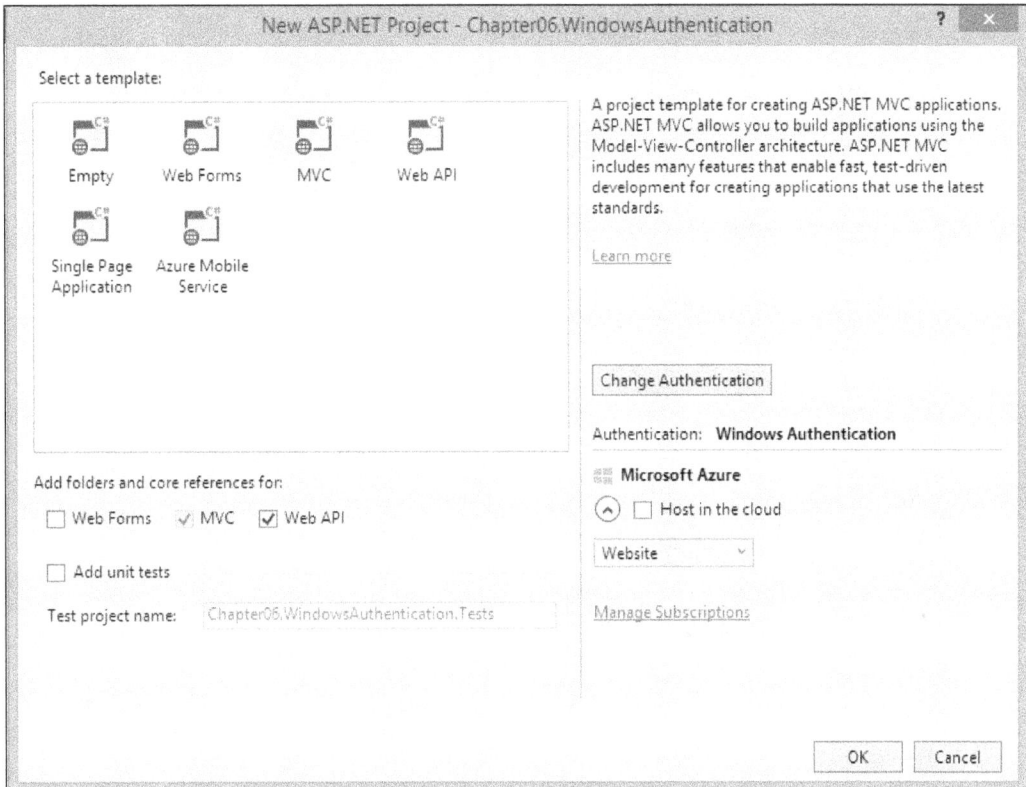

Fig 7 – Select MVC template and check Web API in add folders and core references

8. Under the Models folder, add a class named `Contact.cs` with the following code:

```
namespace Chapter06.FormsAuthentication.Models
{
    public class Contact
    {
        public int Id { get; set; }
        public string Name { get; set; }
        public string Email { get; set; }
        public string Mobile { get; set; }
    }
}
```

9. Add a Web API controller named `ContactsController` with the following code:

```
namespace Chapter06.FormsAuthentication.Api
{
    public class ContactsController : ApiController
    {
        IEnumerable<Contact> contacts = new List<Contact>
        {
            new Contact { Id = 1, Name = "Steve", Email = "steve@
gmail.com", Mobile = "+1(234)35434" },
            new Contact { Id = 2, Name = "Matt", Email = "matt@
gmail.com", Mobile = "+1(234)5654" },
            new Contact { Id = 3, Name = "Mark", Email = "mark@
gmail.com", Mobile = "+1(234)56789" }
        };

        [Authorize]
        // GET: api/Contacts
        public IEnumerable<Contact> Get()
        {
            return contacts;
        }
    }
}
```

10. The `Get()` action in `ContactsController` is decorated with the `[Authorize]` attribute. But in Windows authentication, any request is considered as authenticated request if the client relies on the same domain. So no explicit login process is required to send an authenticated request to call the `Get()` action.

> Note that Windows authentication is configured in the `Web.config` file, as follows:
>
> ```
> <system.web>
>     <authentication mode="Windows" />
> </system.web>
> ```

Difference between Basic Authentication and Windows authentication

Windows authentication authenticates the user by validating the credentials against the user account in a Windows domain.

Basic authentication verifies the credentials that are provided in a form against the user account that is stored in a database.

Enabling Windows authentication in Katana

Katana is a collection of projects to support OWIN with various Microsoft components for `System.Web` and `System.Net.HttpListener`.

We can plug Web API in an OWIN-based application rather than depending on `System.Web` file. This can be achieved by installing the `Microsoft.AspNet.WebApi.Owin` NuGet package that allows adding Web API to middleware pipeline.

Follow the steps to create a console application and enable Windows authentication in Katana:

1. Create **New Project** from the **Start** page in Visual Studio.
2. Select **Visual C# Installed Template** named **Windows Desktop**.
3. Select **Console Application** in the center pane.

4. Name the project as `Chapter06.WindowsAuthenticationKatana` and
   click **OK**:

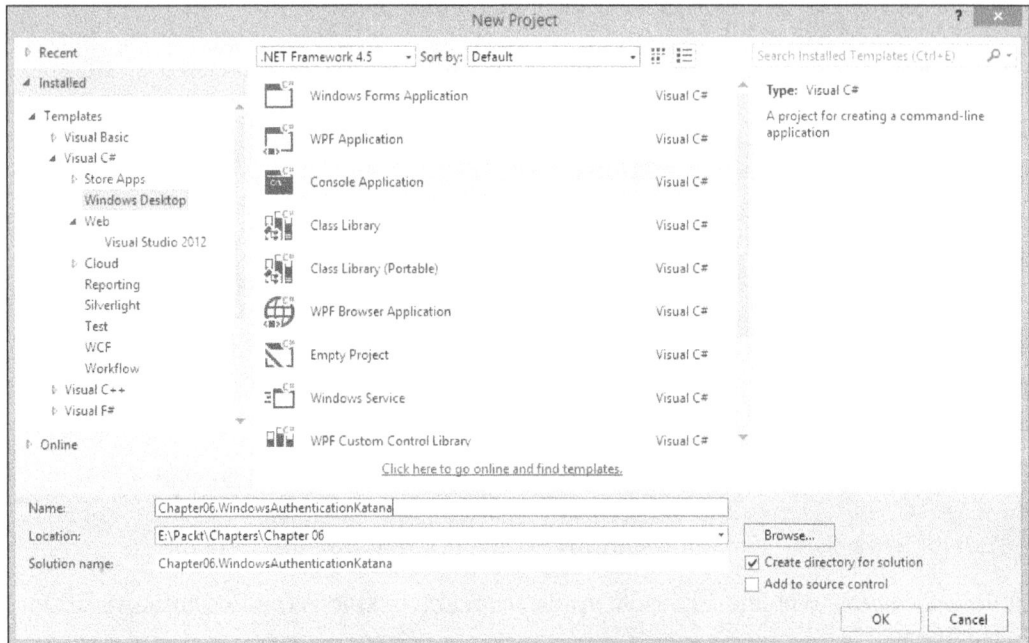

Fig 8 – We have named the Console Application "Chapter06.WindowsAuthenticationKatana"

5. Install **NuGet Package** named **Microsoft.Owin.SelfHost** from **NuGet
   Package Manager**:

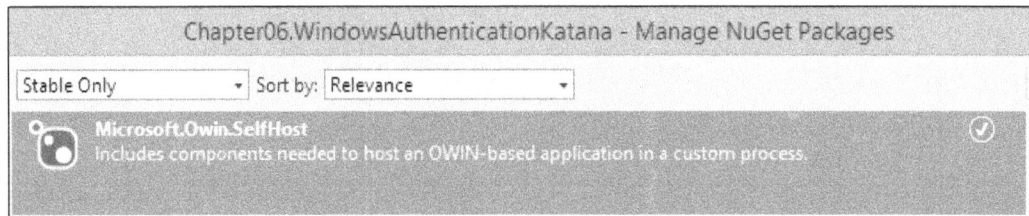

Fig 9 – Install NuGet Package named Microsoft.Owin.SelfHost

6. Add a Startup class with the following code snippet:

```
namespace Chapter06.WindowsAuthenticationKatana
{
    class Startup
    {
        public void Configuration(IAppBuilder app)
        {
            var listener =
```

```
                (HttpListener)app.Properties["System.Net.
HttpListener"];
            listener.AuthenticationSchemes =
                AuthenticationSchemes.
IntegratedWindowsAuthentication;

            app.Run(context =>
            {
                context.Response.ContentType = "text/plain";
                return context.Response.WriteAsync("Hello Packt
Readers!");
            });
        }
    }
}
```

7. Add the following code in the Main function in `Program.cs`, as follows:

```
using (WebApp.Start<Startup>("http://localhost:8001"))
{
        Console.WriteLine("Press any Key to quit Web App.");
        Console.ReadKey();
}
```

8. Now run the application and open `http://localhost:8001/` in the browser, as shown in the following screenshot:

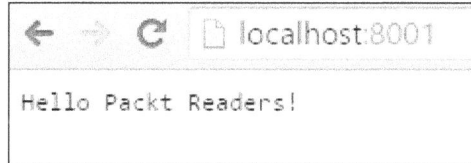

Fig 10 – Open the Web App in a browser

9. If you capture the request using Fiddler, you will notice an Authorization Negotiate entry in the header of the request.

10. Try calling `http://localhost:8001/` in Fiddler and you will get a `401 Unauthorized` response with `WWW-Authenticate` headers, which indicates that the server attaches the `Negotiate` protocol that consumes either Kerberos or NTLM as given in the following:

```
HTTP/1.1 401 Unauthorized
Content-Length: 0
Server: Microsoft-HTTPAPI/2.0
WWW-Authenticate: Negotiate
WWW-Authenticate: NTLM
Date: Tue, 13 Oct 2015 15:43:35 GMT
Proxy-Support: Session-Based-Authentication
```

Summary

Voilà! We just secured our Web API using Forms and Windows authentication.

In this chapter, you learned how Forms authentication works and how it is implemented in Web API.

You also learned about configuring Windows authentication and got to study the advantages and disadvantages of using Windows authentication.

Then you learned about implementing Windows authentication mechanism in Katana.

In the next chapter, let's see how to use external authentication services, such as Facebook and Twitter, to secure Web API.

7
Using External Authentication Services with ASP.NET Web API

This chapter will help you to understand the need for external authentication services to enable OAuth/OpenID and social media authentication.

In this chapter, we will cover the following topics:

- Using OWIN external authentication services
- Implementing Facebook authentication
- Implementing Twitter authentication
- Implementing Google authentication
- Implementing Microsoft authentication
- Discussing authentication

Using OWIN external authentication services

Using external authentication services for authentication reduces the development time that is needed to implement internal authentication mechanisms. Most web users have accounts on social media websites, such as Facebook and Twitter, and other services, such as Microsoft and Google. Using external authentication services saves the time of users to create another account for your web application.

ASP.NET provides built-in support for external authentication services such as Facebook, Twitter, Microsoft, and Google.

Creating an ASP.NET MVC Application

Let's create an ASP.NET MVC application in order to demonstrate how to implement external authentication solutions, as follows:

1. Create New Project from the Start page in Visual Studio.

2. Select Visual C# Installed Template named Web.

3. Select ASP.NET Web Application in the center pane.

4. Name the project as Chapter07.ExternalAuthentication and click **OK**:

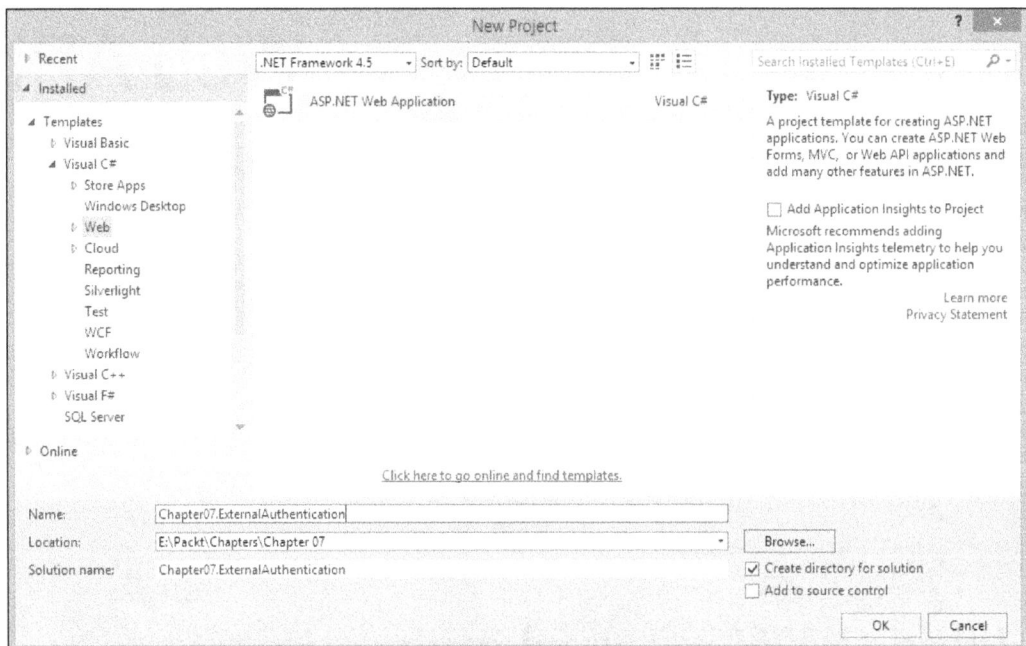

Fig 1 – We have named the ASP.NET Web Application as "Chapter07.ExternalAuthentication"

5. Select the **MVC** template in the **New ASP.NET Project** dialog.

6. Check **Web API** and click **OK** under **Add folders and core references for,** leaving the **Authentication** to **Individual User Accounts**:

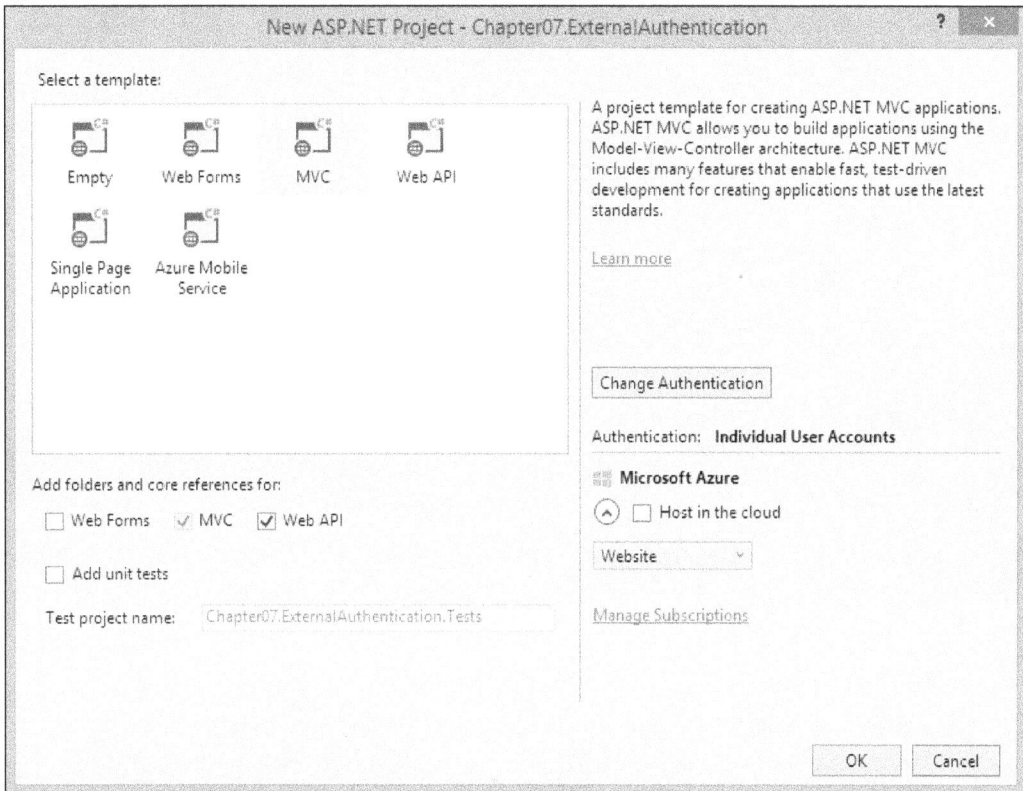

Fig 2 – Select MVC template and check Web API in add folders and core references

7. Add a model class named `Contact.cs` to the Models folder with the following code:

```
namespace Chapter07.ExternalAuthentication.Models
{
    public class Contact
    {
        public int Id { get; set; }
        public string Name { get; set; }
        public string Email { get; set; }
        public string Mobile { get; set; }
    }
}
```

8. Add a Web API controller named `ContactsController` and replace the code with the following code:

```
namespace Chapter07.ExternalAuthentication.Api
{
    public class ContactsController : ApiController
    {
        IEnumerable<Contact> contacts = new List<Contact>
        {
            new Contact { Id = 1, Name = "Steve", Email = "steve@
gmail.com", Mobile = "+1(234)35434" },
            new Contact { Id = 2, Name = "Matt", Email = "matt@
gmail.com", Mobile = "+1(234)5654" },
            new Contact { Id = 3, Name = "Mark", Email = "mark@
gmail.com", Mobile = "+1(234)56789" }
        };

        [Authorize]
        // GET: api/Contacts
        public IEnumerable<Contact> Get()
        {
            return contacts;
        }
    }
}
```

We just created an ASP.NET MVC application and added a Web API controller named `ContactsController` to supply a list of contact details. The `Get` action in `ContactsController` is decorated with the [`Authorize`] attribute and can only be called using an authenticated request. Now let's add external the authentication solutions one by one to authenticate the request.

Implementing Facebook authentication

To apply Facebook authentication services to our application, we first need to create a developer account in Facebook and then, using the developer account, we need to create an application on Facebook. This application will provide us with an app ID and a secret key to enable Facebook authentication in our application. Follow the given steps to get the keys from Facebook:

1. Log in to Facebook using your credentials.

2. Navigate to the Facebook developers website (`https://developers.facebook.com/`).

3. Click the **Register as a Developer** menu item under the **My Apps** menu:

Fig 3 – Select Register as a Developer from the menu

4. Select **Yes** to accept the Facebook Platform Policy and Facebook Privacy Policy and click **Register**, which would successfully register you as a Facebook Developer. You can now add Facebook to your app or website:

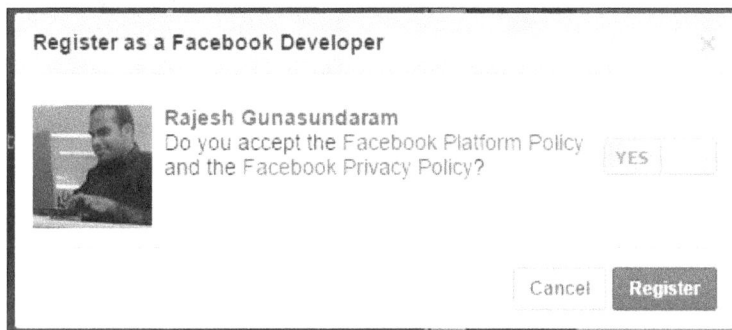

Fig 4 – Click Register to register as a Facebook developer

5. Click **Website** in the **Add a New App** page:

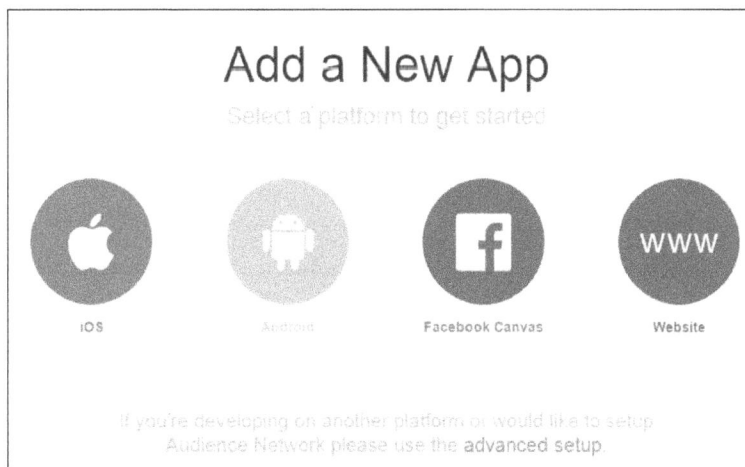

Fig 5 – Select Website in the Add a New App page

6. Click **Skip and Create App ID** on the **Quick Start for Website** page:

Fig 6 – Navigate to the Skip and Create App ID link

7. Provide **Display Name** and **Namespace.** Select **Category** under the model popup dialog. Then click the **Create App ID** button:

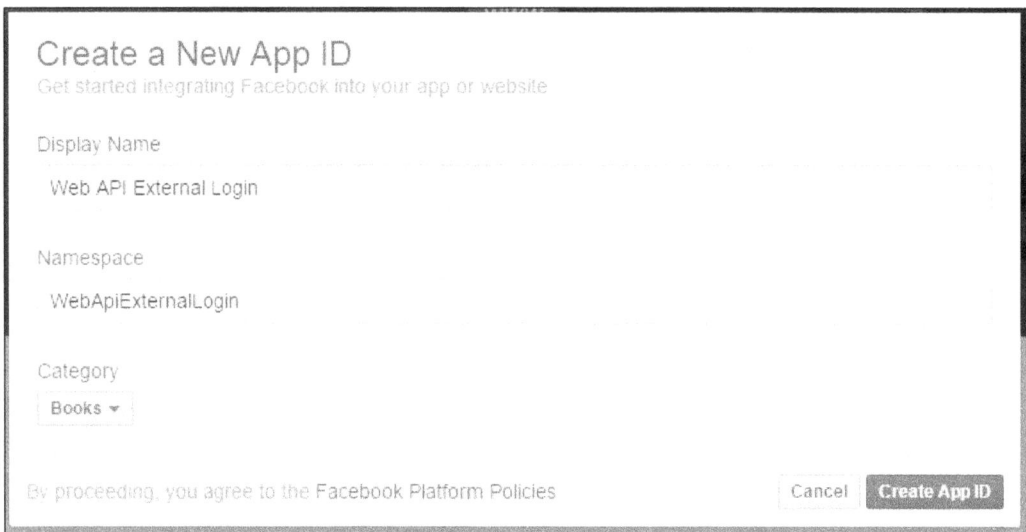

Fig 7 – Navigate to Skip and Create App ID link

8. Confirm the captcha as a security check by entering the text exactly in the same case, since it is case sensitive, and click **Submit**:

Security Check

Can't read the text above?
Try another text or an audio captcha
Text in the box:

UNy7HK|

What's this?

If you think you're seeing this by mistake, please let us know.

Submit   Cancel

Fig 8 – Confirm the captcha for security purposes

9. Now the Dashboard for the created Facebook app will be shown with the details of the **App ID**, **API Version**, and **App Secret key**:

Dashboard

Web API External Login

This app is in development mode and can only be used by app admins, developers and testers [?]

App ID   API Version [?]   App Secret

                          v2.4   ●●●●●●●●   Show

Fig 9 – App ID and Secret key is available under dashboard

10. Navigate to **Settings** and click on **Add Platform**:

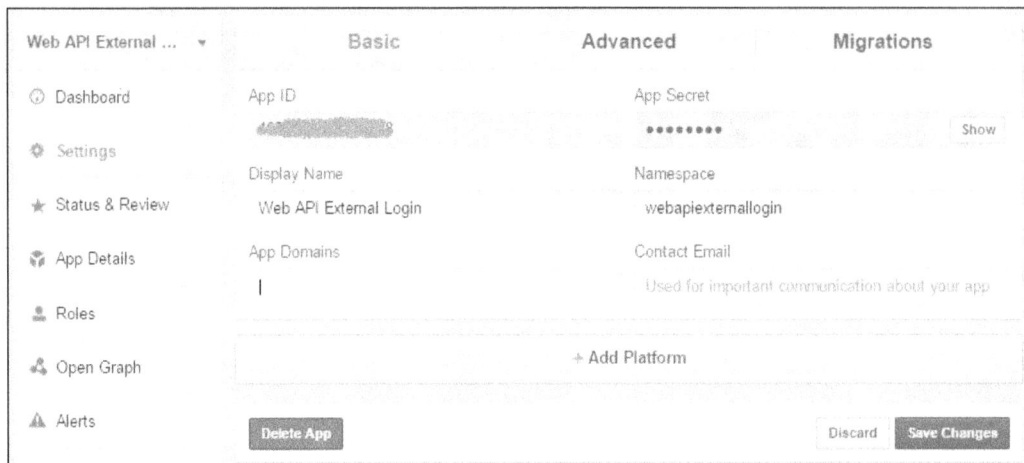

Fig 10 – App ID and Secret key is available under dashboard

11. Click **Website** under the **Select Platform** model popup dialog:

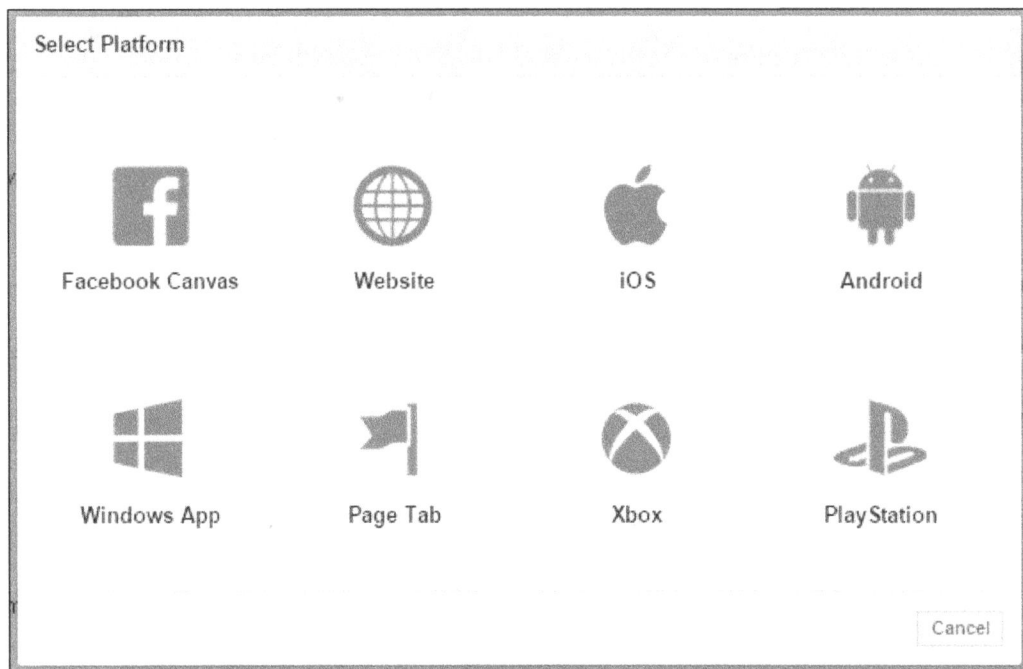

Fig 11 – Select website for the platform

12. Enter your website URL in **Site URL** under the **Website** panel that was added. You can also use localhost URL as **Site URL** during development:

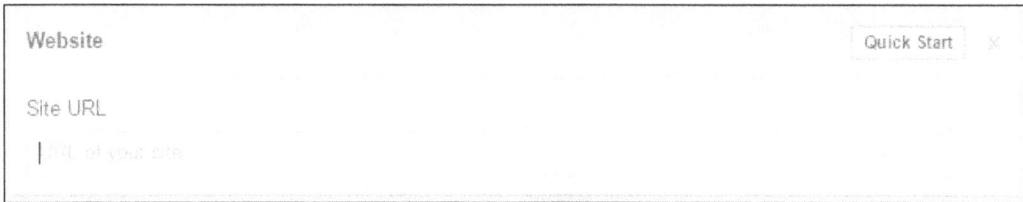

Fig 12 – Provide your application URL

13. Click the **Save Changes** button to save the changes made.

14. Copy the **App ID** and **App Secret Key** values as you need to configure your application code. These values will be passed to the Facebook provider from your website when the user tries to log in using his Facebook account.

15. Exit the Facebook developer site.

16. Open the ASP.NET MVC application that we created in the previous section.

17. Open the `Startup.Auth.cs` class file under the `App_Start` folder.

18. Update the copied **App ID** and **App Secret Key** in the folllowing code under the `ConfigureAuth` method:

```
app.UseFacebookAuthentication(
    appId: "",
    appSecret: "");
```

19. Now, run the application and try to log in using Facebook by clicking the Facebook button. Your website will be redirected to Facebook in order to authenticate the login request:

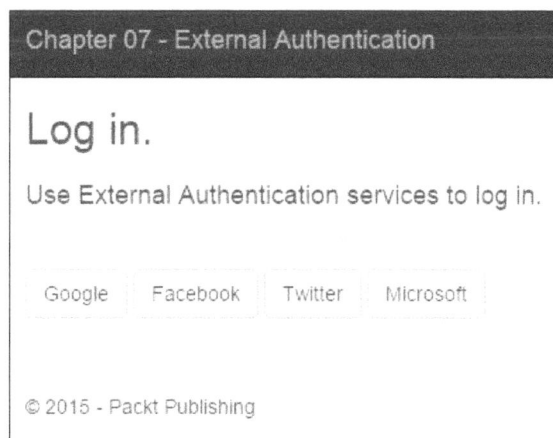

Fig 13 – Click on Facebook to authenticate the user to access your application

20. Facebook will confirm with the user whether they are fine with the app that may access the public profile information. Your public profile includes name, profile picture, age range, gender, language, country, and other public information:

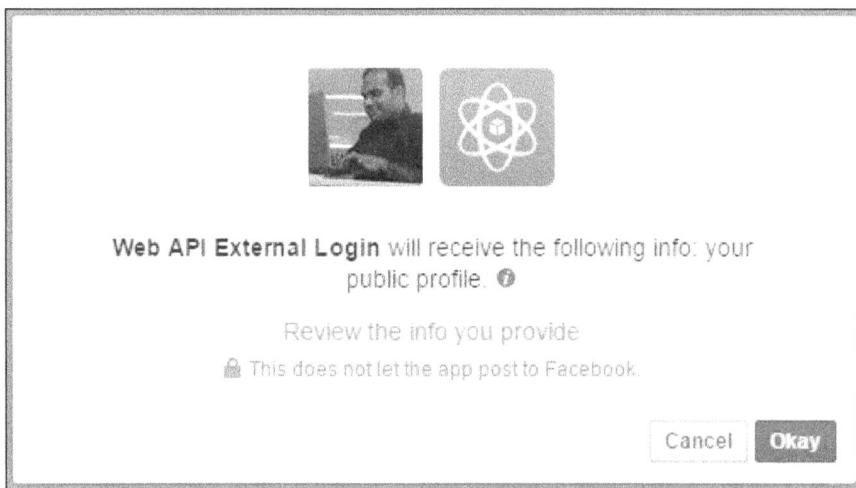

Fig 14 – Confirm to access your profile information

21. Clicking **Okay** will redirect you back to the application and you will be asked to provide your email ID in order to register the user who has logged in via Facebook, by associating his Facebook account. The redirect happens as we supplied a redirect URL for our application:

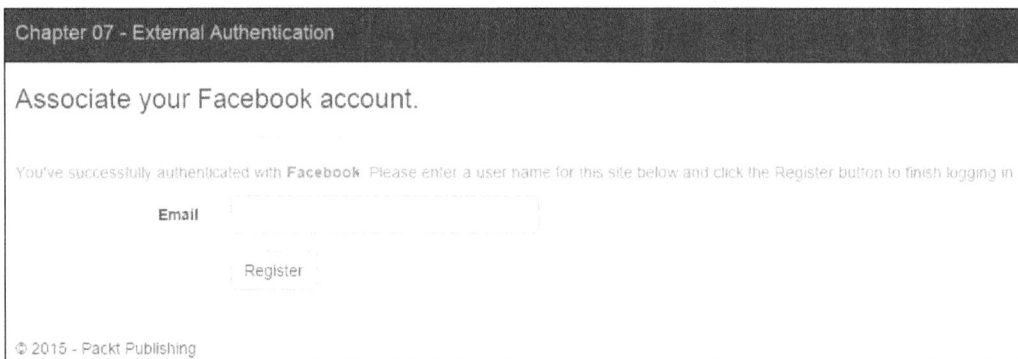

Chapter 07 - External Authentication

Associate your Facebook account.

You've successfully authenticated with **Facebook**. Please enter a user name for this site below and click the Register button to finish logging in.

Email

Register

© 2015 - Packt Publishing

Fig 15 – Associate your Facebook account by registering your email id

Implementing Twitter authentication

As we implemented Facebook authentication, we also need to create a Twitter developer account and need to supply consumer key and consumer secret value from our application to Twitter for authentication.

Follow the given steps to get the consumer key and secret value from the Twitter developer account for your application:

1. Log in to your Twitter account (`https://twitter.com/`).
2. Navigate to the Twitter developer site (`https://dev.twitter.com/`).
3. Scroll down to the footer and click **Manage Your Apps** under the **Tools** section.
4. Click the **Create New App** button in the redirected page:

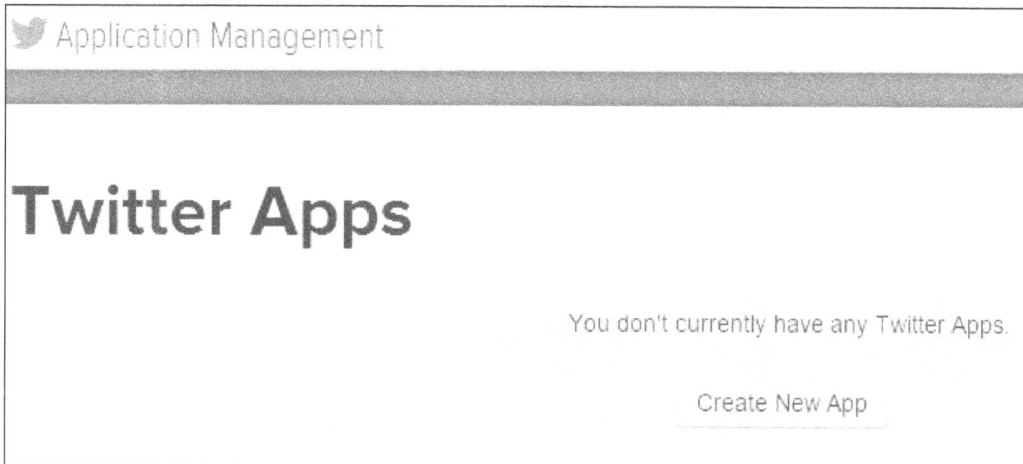

Fig 16 – Create your Twitter Application

5. Provide your Application Details such as **Name**, **Description**, **Website**, and **Callback URL**. Tick **agree** to the developer agreement in the **Create an application** page. The Callback URL is the URL of our application that Twitter needs to redirect to after the successful authentication:

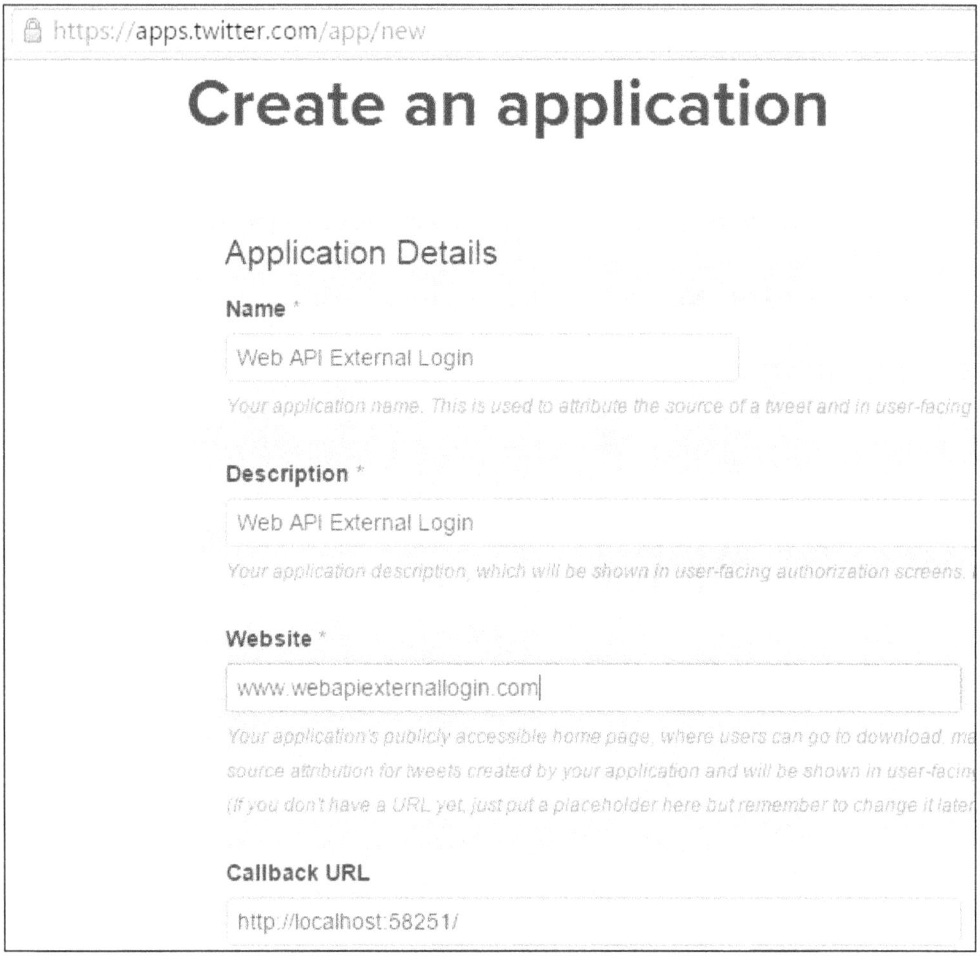

Fig 17 – Providing details to create an application

6. Click the **Create your Twitter** application button.

7. You can find the **consumer key** and **secret values** by clicking **manage keys and access tokens** under the **Application Settings** section on the **Details** tab of the created application. Copy **consumer key** and **secret values**.

8. Open the `Startup.Auth.cs` class file under the **App_Start** folder.

9. Update the copied **Consumer Key** and **Consumer Secret** values in the following code under `ConfigureAuth` method:

```
app.UseTwitterAuthentication(
            consumerKey: "",
            consumerSecret: "");
```

10. Run your application and click on the **Twitter** button in the following page to log in using Twitter:

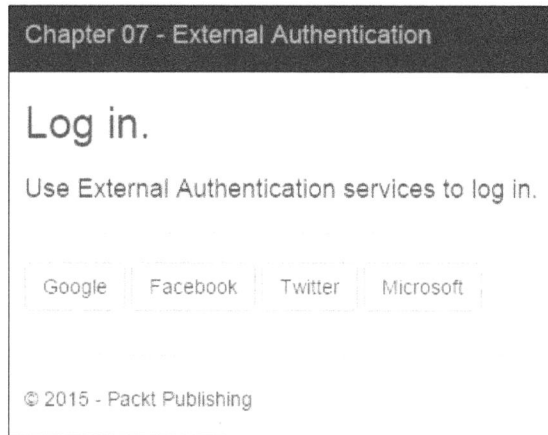

Fig 18 – Click Twitter to authenticate the user

11. Your application will redirect to Twitter for authentication. Click **Sign In** to authorize the Twitter app to use your account and authenticate the access to your application:

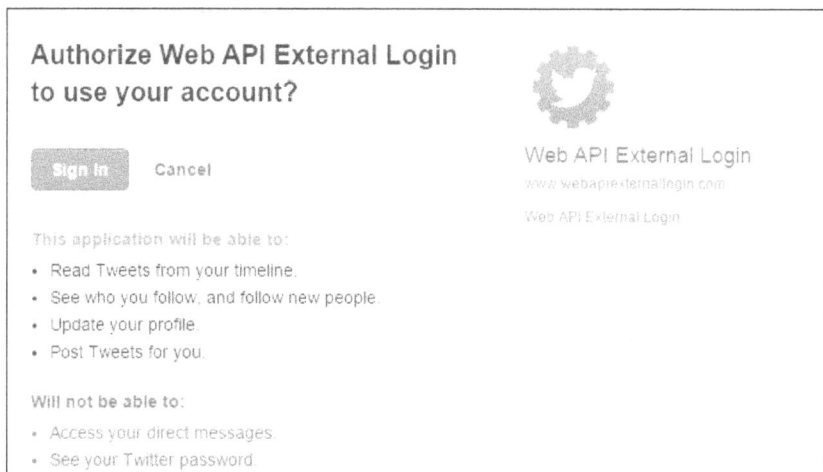

Fig 19 – Authorizing your application by clicking sign in

12. You need to provide your email ID to register and associate your Twitter account:

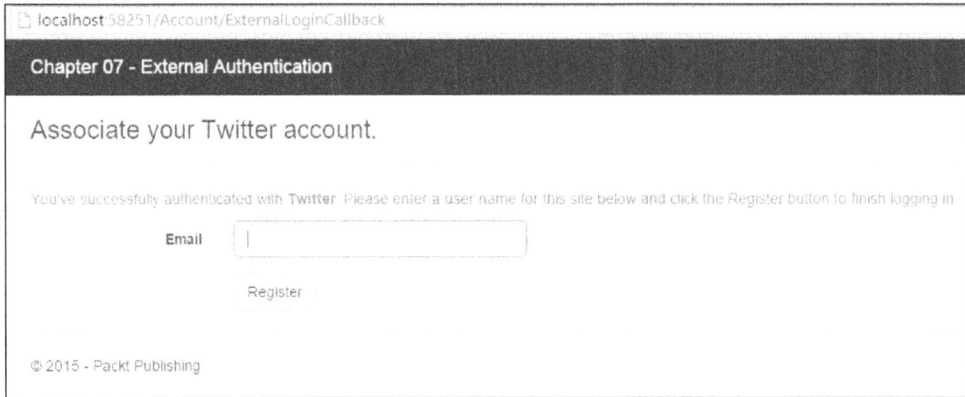

Fig 20 – Associating Twitter application with your application profile

13. Exit the Twitter site.

Implementing Google authentication

So far we have seen how to integrate external authentication using social media websites such as Facebook and Twitter. Now let's see how to integrate Google authentication. We need to create a project and a create client ID and secret key in the Google developer console and this client ID and secret key should be configured in our application.

Follow the given steps to get the client ID and secret key value from the Google developer console for your application:

1. Log in to your Google account (https://www.google.com/).

2. Open the Google developer console site (https://console.developers. google.com/).

3. Click **Create Project**:

Fig 21 –Creating Project in Google developer console

4. Enter the **Project Name** and click the **Create** button:

Fig 22 – Providing the project name and create

5. Click **APIs & auth | APIs** and enable **Google+ API**.

6. Click **APIs & auth | Credentials** and select the **OAuth consent screen** tab. Provide the **Project Name** and **Save**:

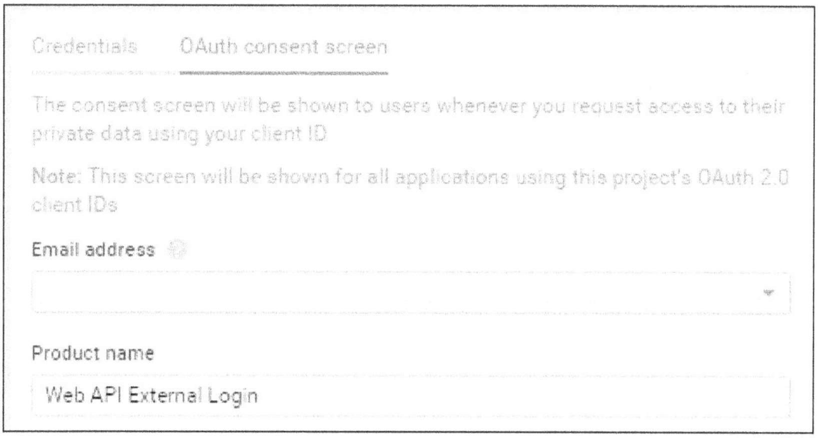

Fig 23 – Providing your email address

7. Select **OAuth 2.0 client ID** under **Add credentials**:

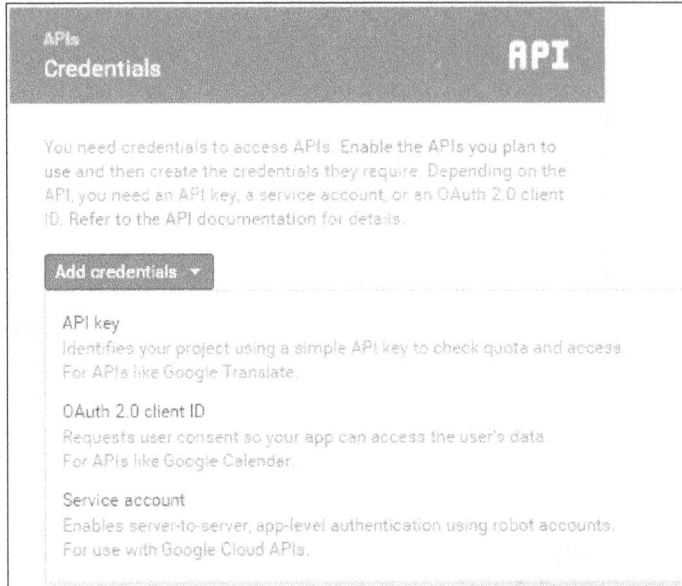

Fig 24 – Select API key in the add credentials button dropdown. This screenshot was taken by September 2015

8. Create client ID by selecting **web application** as **Application Type** and providing **authorized JavaScript origins** and **redirect URIs**:

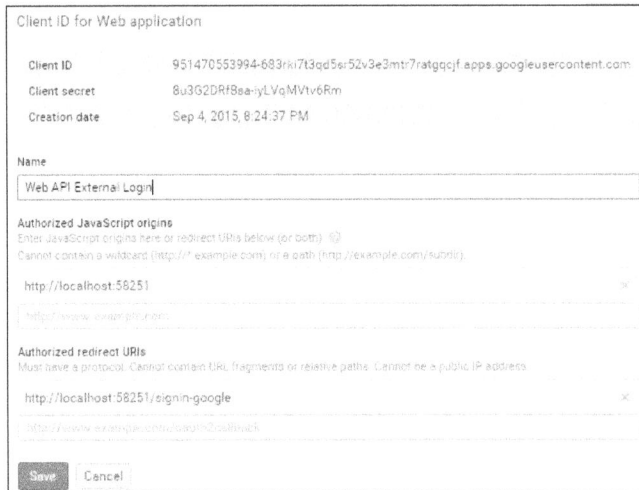

Fig 25 – Configure authorized application type, JavaScript origins and redirect URIs

9. The **client ID** and **secret key** will be shown on a modal popup, as follows:

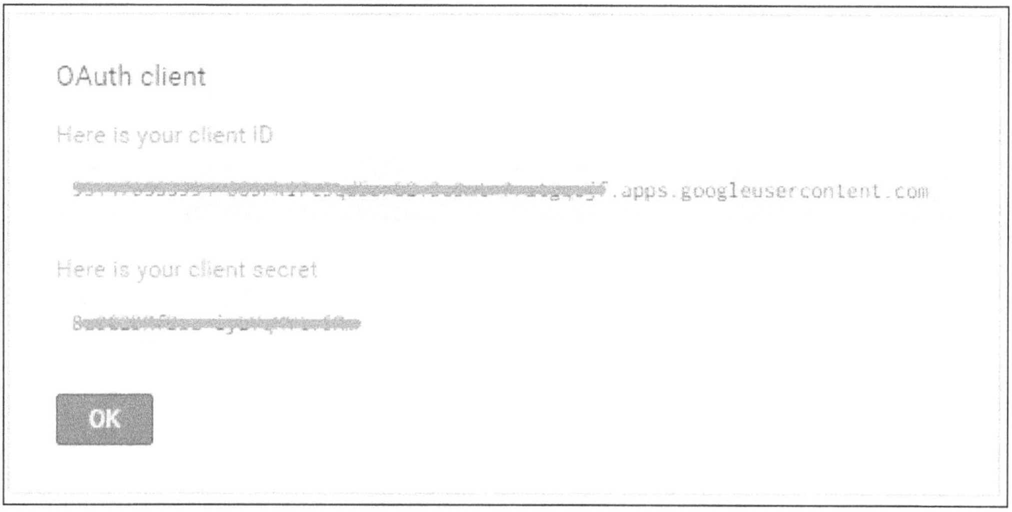

OAuth client

Here is your client ID

██.apps.googleusercontent.com

Here is your client secret

████████████████████████████████

OK

Fig 26 – Copy the Client ID and Secret key value

10. Copy **Client ID** and **Secret key**.

11. Open the `Startup.Auth.cs` class file under the **App_Start** folder.

12. Update the copied **Client ID** and **Secret Key** values in the following code under the `ConfigureAuth` method:

```
app.UseGoogleAuthentication(new GoogleOAuth2AuthenticationOptions()
        {
              ClientId = "",
              ClientSecret = ""
        });
```

13. Run the web application and log in using Google from the external authentication service login page.

14. The web application will be redirected to Google for authentication. Click **Allow** to authorize the application to access the user profile and authenticate using your Google account:

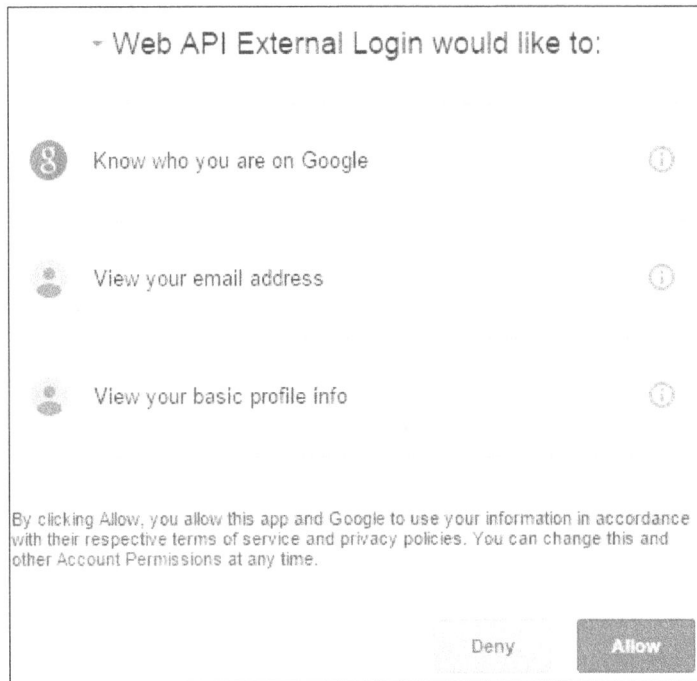

Fig 27 – Provide details to create an application

15. You need to provide your email ID to register and associate your Google account:

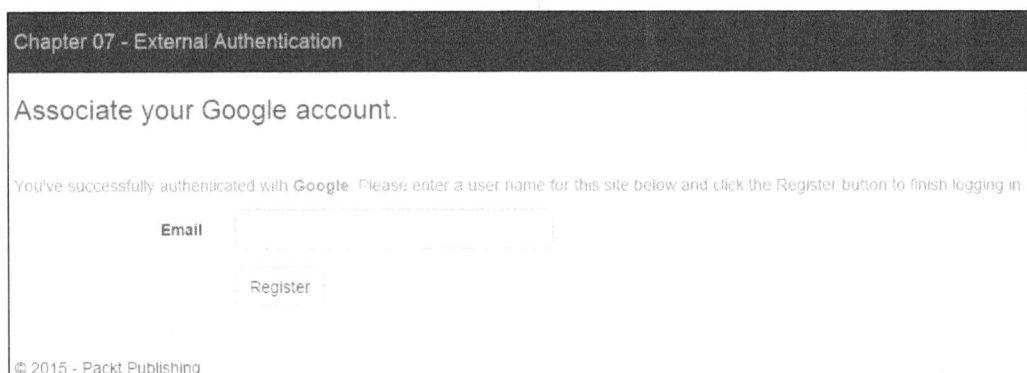

Fig 28 – Associate your Google account by registering your email id

16. Exit the Google site.

Implementing Microsoft authentication

Microsoft authentication is like utilizing your end users' enterprise accounts to authenticate them. We need to create an application and configure redirect URL. Then copy the client ID and secret key from app settings in the Microsoft developer account and configure them in our application code.

Follow the given steps to get the client ID and secret key value from the Microsoft developer portal for your application:

Log to your Microsoft account (`https://www.live.com/`).

1. Navigate to the Microsoft developer center site (`https://account.live. com/developers/applications/`).

2. Provide the **Application name** and click the **I accept** button:

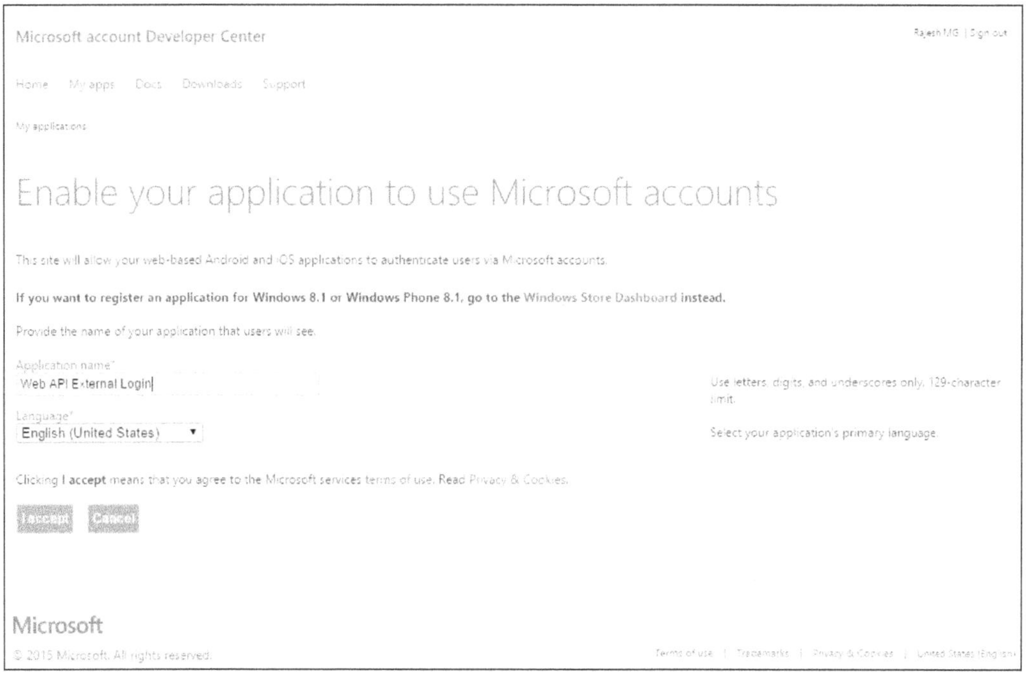

Fig 29 – Enable your application to use Microsoft accounts

3. Click on **API Settings** and configure **Redirect URLs**:

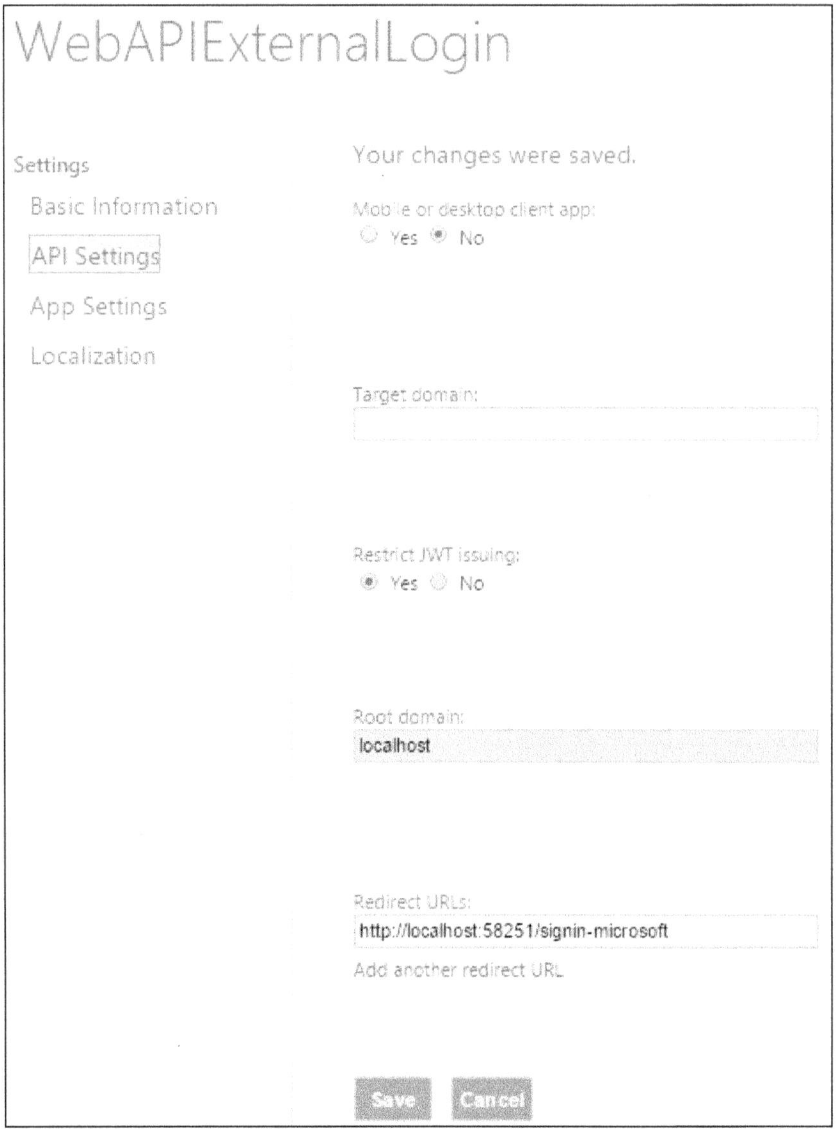

Fig 30 – Configure redirect URL for your application

4. Click **App Settings** and copy the **Client ID** and **Client Secret** value:

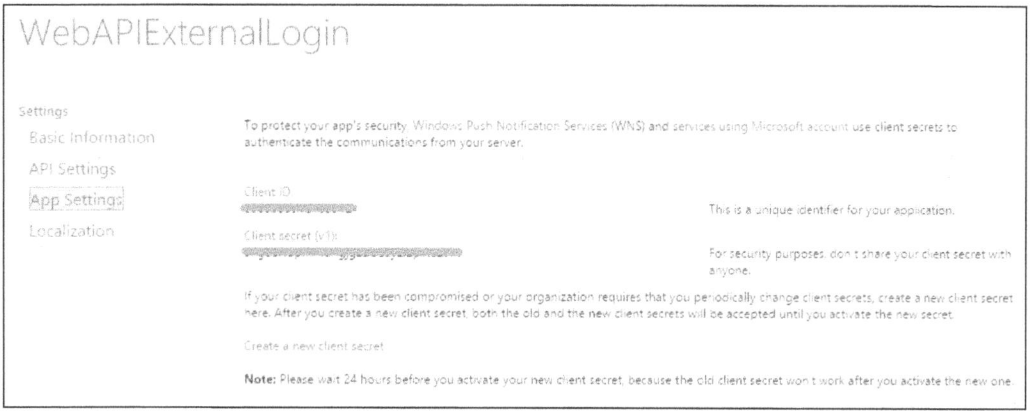

Fig 31 – Copy Client ID and Secret Key values

5. Open the `Startup.Auth.cs` class file under the **App_Start** folder.

6. Update the copied **Client ID** and **Secret Key** values in the following code under `ConfigureAuth` method:

```
app.UseMicrosoftAccountAuthentication(
                clientId: "",
                clientSecret: "");
```

7. Run the web application and log in using Microsoft account from the external authentication service login page.

8. On clicking the Microsoft button for login, your application will redirect to Microsoft Live for authentication. Click **Yes** to authorize the application and authenticate the user that is using your Microsoft account:

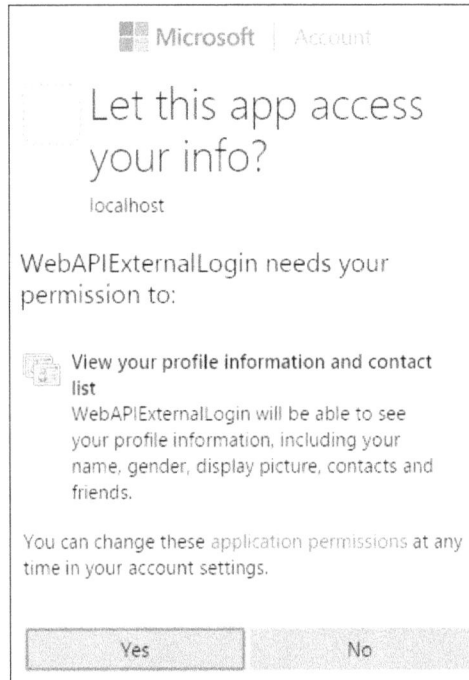

Fig 32 – Allow your application to access user info from a Microsoft account

9. You need to provide your email ID to register and associate your Microsoft account:

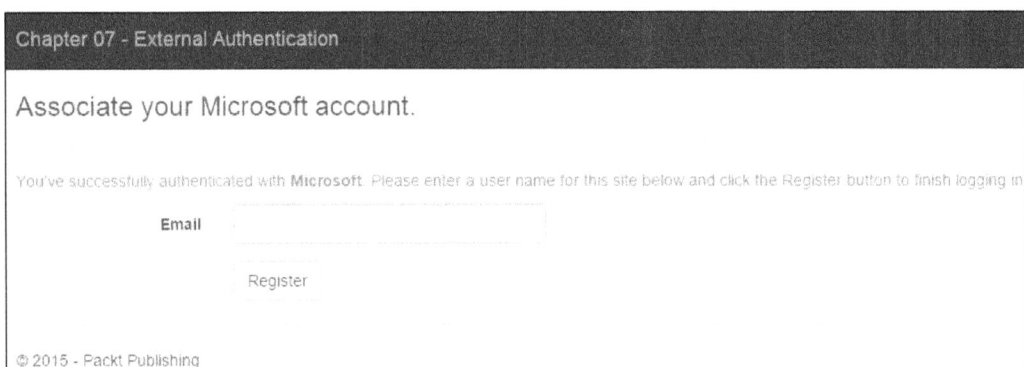

Fig 33 – Associate your Microsoft account by registering your email

10. Exit the Microsoft site.

Discussing authentication

In the previous sections, we have seen how the external authentication is carried out. It all starts with registering the user details that are retrieved from the external authentication providers. On successful registration of the user's details with our application, we don't need to store the user details again in our application again.

This time the external authentication providers will not ask the permission of users in order to enable access to their public profile information as the user has already given the permission to our application. So, the external authentication providers will just authenticate the user and our application will bypass the registration process for the existing users.

Summary

Voila! We just secured our Web API using the external authentication mechanisms.

In this chapter, you learned about OWIN external authentication and how to use it in order to secure our Web API.

You also learned how to register as a developer on external authentication services such as Facebook, Twitter, Google, and Microsoft and create an application there to get client ID and secret key and consumer ID and secret key respectively.

Then you learned how to configure the ID and secret keys that are copied from external authentication services in our source code in order to implement the external authentication in our application.

Finally, we ran the application and saw the working of external authentication in action.

In the next chapter, let's learn how to protect our Web API from cross-site request forgery attack.

Let's prepare for the attack!

8
Avoiding Cross-Site Request Forgery Attacks in Web API

This chapter will help you in avoiding **Cross-Site Request Forgery** (**CSRF**) in ASP. NET Web API. Using an API key-based authentication or a more sophisticated mechanism, such as OAuth, to avoid CSRF attacks.

In this chapter, we will cover the following topics:

- What is a CSRF attack?
- Anti-forgery tokens using HTML Form or Razor View
- Anti-forgery tokens using AJAX

What is a CSRF attack?

As given in Wikipedia (`https://en.wikipedia.org/wiki/Cross-site_request_ forgery/`), Cross-site request forgery (CSRF or XSRF), also known as a one-click attack or session riding, is a type of malicious exploit of a website whereby unauthorized commands are transmitted from a user that the website trusts. Unlike cross-site scripting (XSS), which exploits the trust a user has for a particular site, CSRF exploits the trust that a site has in a user's browser.

In simple terms, this type of attack is made by a malicious site on sending a request to the user that has logged into a vulnerable site.

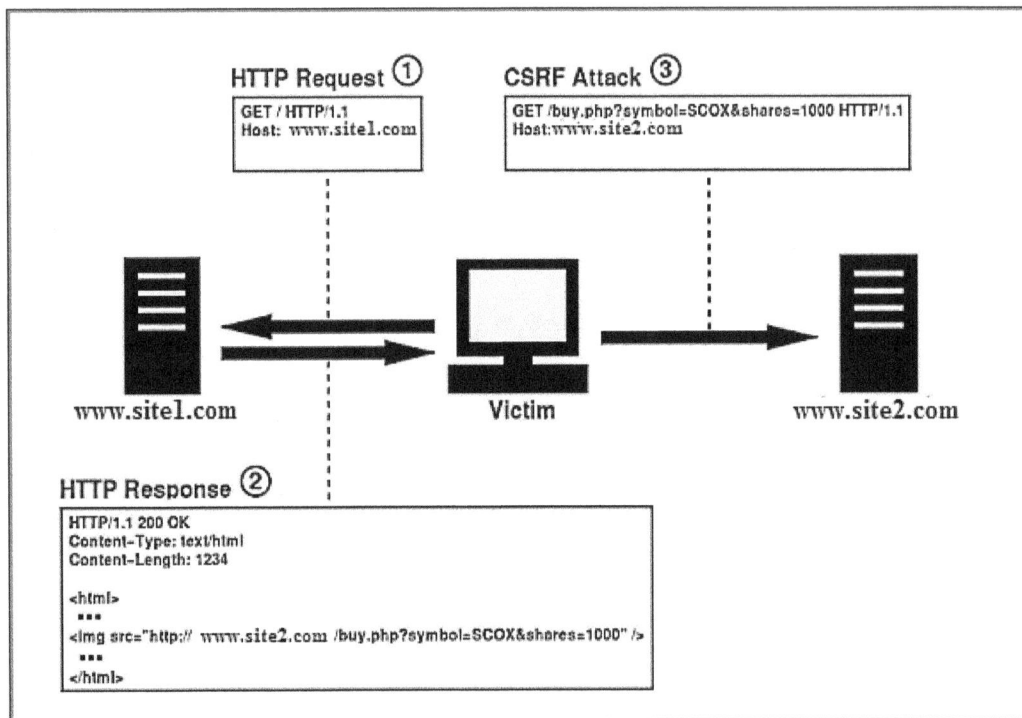

Fig 1 – CSRF attack illustrated in the image

Anti-forgery tokens using HTML Form or Razor View

Anti-forgery tokens or request verification tokens are used in ASP.NET MVC to avoid CSRF attack. Anti-forgery tokens or request verification tokens help in preventing the CSRF attacks. The .Net framework has a built-in support to create and validate anti-forgery tokens. The @Html.AntiForgeryToken() method in the MVC Razor engine creates the anti-forgery tokens. The validation of an anti-forgery token can be achieved by decorating the controller or action with the [ValidateAntiForgeryToken] attribute.

How does an Anti-forgery token work?

Let's see how the server accepts or rejects a request based on the anti-forgery token. Given in the following are the steps that are involved in making the anti-forgery token work:

1. The client sends a request for an MVC view with the form.

2. The server returns the requested view along with two tokens, one sent via cookie and other sent by setting to a hidden field in the form of the view.

3. These two tokens will be passed back to the server when the client submits the form in the `view`.

4. The server looks for these two tokens in the successive request and if it doesn't find the tokens, then the request will be rejected.

It is necessary to protect the anti-forgery token as we protect authentication tokens. So it is the best practice to use SSL. Refer to *Chapter 2, Enabling SSL for ASP.NET Web API* to see how to enable **SSL** for ASP.NET Web API.

Anti-forgery tokens using AJAX

It is very common to use AJAX to post data to or get data from the server. An AJAX request sends the JSON data to server. It doesn't send the HTML form data. To achieve sending the token via an AJAX post, we need to use the custom HTTP header. Using Razor syntax, we can generate the tokens by calling the `AntiForgery.GetTokens()` method and attach it to the request as given in the following code:

```
<script>
    @functions{
        public string GetAntiForgeryTokenValue ()
        {
            string tokenInCookie, tokenInForm;
            AntiForgery.GetTokens(null, out tokenInCookie, out
tokenInForm);
            return tokenInCookie + ":" + tokenInForm;
        }
    }

    $.ajax("/api/contacts", {
            type: "get",
            headers: {
                'AntiForgeryToken': '@GetAntiForgeryTokenValue()'
                },
```

```
                    success: function (result) {
                        alert(JSON.stringify(result));
                    },
                    error: function (XMLHttpRequest, textStatus,
    errorThrown) {
                        alert(errorThrown + " Error");
                    }
                });
    </script>
```

The tokens that are passed via AJAX should be extracted when the request is processed. Then the extracted tokens have to be validated using the AntiForgery.Validate method as given in the following code snippet. The AntiForgery.Validate method throws an exception if the tokens are invalid in the request, as follows:

```
void ValidateToken(HttpRequestMessage request)
{
    string tokenInCookie = "";
    string tokenInForm = "";

    IEnumerable<string> tokenHeaders;
    if (request.Headers.TryGetValues("AntiForgeryToken", out
tokenHeaders))
    {
        var tokens = tokenHeaders.First().Split(':');
        if (tokens.Length == 2)
        {
            tokenInCookie = tokens[0].Trim();
            tokenInForm = tokens[1].Trim();
        }
    }
    AntiForgery.Validate(tokenInCookie, tokenInForm);
}
```

We can implement an authorization filter for Web API and decorate it to action in order to validate the anti-forgery token before invoking the action. The following code snippet shows one such authorization filter:

```
namespace Chapter08.AntiForgeryToken.Filters
{
    [AttributeUsage(AttributeTargets.Method | AttributeTargets.Class,
AllowMultiple = false, Inherited = true)]
    public class ValidateAntiForgeryTokenAttribute : FilterAttribute,
IAuthorizationFilter
    {
```

```
      public Task<HttpResponseMessage> ExecuteAuthorizationF
ilterAsync(HttpActionContext actionContext, CancellationToken
cancellationToken, Func<Task<HttpResponseMessage>> continuation)
        {
            try
            {
                string tokenInCookie = "";
                string tokenInForm = "";

                IEnumerable<string> AntiForgeryTokenValue;
                if (actionContext.Request.Headers.TryGetValues("AntiFo
rgeryToken", out AntiForgeryTokenValue))
                {
                    var antiForgeryTokens = AntiForgeryTokenValue.
First().Split(':');
                    if (antiForgeryTokens.Length == 2)
                    {
                        tokenInCookie = antiForgeryTokens [0].Trim();
                        tokenInForm = antiForgeryTokens [1].Trim();
                    }
                }
                AntiForgery.Validate(tokenInCookie, tokenInForm);
            }
            catch (System.Web.Mvc.HttpAntiForgeryException e)
            {
                actionContext.Response = new HttpResponseMessage
                {
                    StatusCode = HttpStatusCode.Forbidden,
                    RequestMessage = actionContext.ControllerContext.
Request
                };
                var response = new TaskCompletionSource<HttpResponseM
essage>();
                response.SetResult(actionContext.Response);
                return response.Task;
            }
            return continuation();
        }
    }
}
```

CSRF attacks will be refused with the 403 Forbidden error by the server.

Summary

Short and sweet, isn't it? You just learned how to protect our Web API from cross-site request forgery attacks.

You also learned about what is meant by a CSRF attack and how it impacts our Web API.

Then you learned about implementing anti-forgery tokens using HTML form and AJAX.

In the next chapter, let's see how to enable cross-origin resource sharing in Web API.

Let's get down to the origins!

9

Enabling Cross-Origin Resource Sharing (CORS) in ASP.NET Web API

This chapter will help you in learning how to enable CORS in your Web API application.

In this chapter, we will cover the following topics:

- What is CORS?
- How CORS works
- Setting the allowed origins
- Setting the allowed HTTP methods
- Setting the allowed request headers
- Setting the allowed response headers
- Passing credentials in cross-origin requests
- Enabling CORS at various scopes

What is CORS?

According to the same-origin policy, browser security avoids any AJAX requests from one domain to your Web API on another domain in order to prevent a malicious site from reading sensitive data or posting it to another site. But, in some cases, you may need to enable other domains to call your Web API. This is where CORS comes into the picture.

Cross-Origin Resource Sharing (CORS) allows a server to ignore the same-origin policy as per the configuration. CORS enables server to provide restricted access to its resources.

How CORS works

Cross-origin resource sharing design presents various HTTP headers, such as Origin and Access-Control-Allow-Origin. These headers will be set by a browser for cross-origin requests, if it supports CORS.

Let's try to access the following Web API method that is not configured to support CORS:

```
// GET: api/Contacts/id
public Contact Get(int id)
{
        return contacts.FirstOrDefault(x => x.Id == id);
}
```

Accessing this method from a different domain will lead to the following error:

```
XMLHttpRequest cannot load http://localhost:53858/api/contacts/1.
No 'Access-Control-Allow-Origin' header is present on the requested
resource. Origin 'http://localhost:53870' is therefore not allowed
access.
```

We need to pass some special headers such as Origin header in the request to Web API methods that are configured with CORS. The following code snippet shows one such method in Web API:

```
[EnableCors(origins: "http://localhost:53870", headers: "*", methods:
"*")]
// GET: api/Contacts
public IEnumerable<Contact> Get()
{
    return contacts;
}
```

To access this method, client needs to pass its domain in Origin header so that it will be verified by the Web API server. The following is the sample HTTP request with Origin header that has the information for the domain that is sending this request:

```
GET http://localhost:53858/api/contacts HTTP/1.1
Host: localhost:53858
Connection: keep-alive
Accept: */*
```

```
Origin: http://localhost:53870
User-Agent: Mozilla/5.0 (Windows NT 6.3; WOW64) AppleWebKit/537.36
(KHTML, like Gecko) Chrome/45.0.2454.85 Safari/537.36
Referer: http://localhost:53870/
Accept-Encoding: gzip, deflate, sdch
Accept-Language: en-GB,en-US;q=0.8,en;q=0.6
```

The sample HTTP response from server that supports CORS and allows the request is given in the following:

```
HTTP/1.1 200 OK
Cache-Control: no-cache
Pragma: no-cache
Content-Type: application/json; charset=utf-8
Expires: -1
Server: Microsoft-IIS/8.0
Access-Control-Allow-Origin: http://localhost:53870
X-AspNet-Version: 4.0.30319
X-Powered-By: ASP.NET
Date: Fri, 04 Sep 2015 05:08:14 GMT
Content-Length: 218

[{"Id":1,"Name":"Steve","Email":"steve@gmail.com","Mobile":"+1(
234)35434"},{"Id":2,"Name":"Matt","Email":"matt@gmail.com","Mob
ile":"+1(234)5654"},{"Id":3,"Name":"Mark","Email":"mark@gmail.
com","Mobile":"+1(234)56789"}]
```

As you can see in the preceding response, the Web API server acknowledges the client domain by sending the Access-Control-Allow-Origin header with the allowed domains in response.

Setting the allowed origins

We need to supply the comma separated list of domains in the origins parameter of the [EnableCors] attribute as given in the following code snippet:

```
[EnableCors(origins: " http://localhost:53870, http://
localhost:53871", headers: "*", methods: "*")]
```

As you can see, this CORS configuration only allows AJAX requests from two domains, http://localhost:53870/ and http://localhost:53871/, and rejects any requests from other domains. We can also make CORS accept any requests from all domains by passing a "*" wildcard value as follows:

```
[EnableCors(origins: "*", headers: "*", methods: "*")]
```

It is advisable to reconsider before applying the "*" wildcard value to origins, as it will allow any domain to make AJAX requests to your Web API.

Setting the allowed HTTP methods

We can also restrict the HTTP methods in CORS. This can be achieved by supplying a comma separated list of HTTP methods that are allowed to the [EnableCors] attribute's methods parameter as given in the following:

```
[EnableCors(origins: "http://localhost:53870", headers: "*", methods:
"get,post")]
public class ContactsController : ApiController
    {
        IEnumerable<Contact> contacts = new List<Contact>
        {
            new Contact { Id = 1, Name = "Steve", Email = "steve@
gmail.com", Mobile = "+1(234)35434" },
            new Contact { Id = 2, Name = "Matt", Email = "matt@gmail.
com", Mobile = "+1(234)5654" },
            new Contact { Id = 3, Name = "Mark", Email = "mark@gmail.
com", Mobile = "+1(234)56789" }
        };


        // GET: api/Contacts
        public IEnumerable<Contact> Get()
        {
            return contacts;
        }

        // GET: api/Contacts/id
        public Contact Get(int id)
        {
            return contacts.FirstOrDefault(x => x.Id == id);
        }
    }
```

The preceding code only allows GET and POST HTTP methods. We can also enable to allow all HTTP methods by passing a "*" wildcard value to methods.

Setting the allowed request headers

Sometimes, browsers send a prerequest before sending an actual request in order to verify CORS. Such prerequests will use the HTTP OPTIONS method and the request will have the following access control request headers:

- Access-Control-Request-Method
- Access-Control-Request-Headers

The HTTP action method name that is applied on the actual request is supplied to Access-Control-Request-Method and the list of comma separated headers that is applied on the actual request is supplied to Access-Control-Request-Headers. The following sample request is one such prerequest:

```
OPTIONS http://localhost:53858/api/contacts HTTP/1.1
Host: localhost:53858
Accept: */*
Origin: http://localhost:53870
Access-Control-Request-Method: PUT
Access-Control-Request-Headers: accept, x-my-custom-header
Accept-Encoding: gzip, deflate
User-Agent: Mozilla/5.0 (compatible; MSIE 10.0; Windows NT 6.2; WOW64;
Trident/6.0)
Content-Length: 0
```

Now, the server will respond with the information as to whether it can allow the HTTP method and headers in the special headers of the prerequest for the actual request.

Here in the prerequest, the browser queried the server as to whether it can allow the HTTP method PUT and the request headers such as accept and x-my-custom-header. The following response from the server confirms that it can allow the requested method and headers:

```
HTTP/1.1 200 OK
Cache-Control: no-cache
Pragma: no-cache
Content-Length: 0
Access-Control-Allow-Origin: http://localhost:53870
Access-Control-Allow-Headers: x-my-custom-header
Access-Control-Allow-Methods: PUT
Date: Sun, 30 Aug 2013 05:56:22 IST
```

How is the server configured to allow certain request headers? This will be configured in the headers parameter of the [EnableCors] attribute as given in the following:

```
[EnableCors(origins: "http://localhost:53870",
    headers: "accept,content-type,origin,x-my-header", methods:
"put")]
```

> Note that if any specific custom headers are
> configured, then it is a good practice to include at
> least "accept", "content-type", and "origin", along
> with the custom headers.

Setting the allowed response headers

- There are some default headers that are available in response and is made available by the browsers. Such default headers are Content-Type, Content-Language, Cache-Control, Expires, Pragma, and Last-Modified. These are called simple response headers.

- However, in some scenarios, you may want to expose some special headers in the response. To achieve this, CORS facilitates a parameter named exposedHeaders in the [EnableCors] attribute.

- For example, let's set a special header named "X-Custom-Header" in the response. As this is a special header, it will not be exposed by browsers in a cross-origin request by default. In order to enable the browser to expose this special header, we need to set the header "X-Custom-Header" in the exposedHeaders parameter in the [EnableCors] attribute as given in the following code snippet:

```
[EnableCors(origins: "*", headers: "*", methods: "*",
exposedHeaders: "X-Custom-Header")]
public class ContactsController : ApiController
    {
        IEnumerable<Contact> contacts = new List<Contact>
        {
            new Contact { Id = 1, Name = "Steve", Email = "steve@
gmail.com", Mobile = "+1(234)35434" },
            new Contact { Id = 2, Name = "Matt", Email = "matt@
gmail.com", Mobile = "+1(234)5654" },
            new Contact { Id = 3, Name = "Mark", Email = "mark@
gmail.com", Mobile = "+1(234)56789" }
        };
```

```
       // GET: api/Contacts
       public HttpResponseMessage Get()
       {
var response = new HttpResponseMessage()
       {
            Content = contacts
       };
response.Headers.Add("X-Custom-Header",
"ContactCustomHeaderValue");
            return response;
       }
   }
```

Passing credentials in cross-origin requests

Browsers don't pass credentials such as cookies and HTTP authentication schemes by default in cross-origin requests. To enable passing credentials in cross-origin requests from the client, the client has to set XMLHttpRequest.withCredentials to true as given in the following:

```
$.ajax({
    type: 'get',
    url: ' http://localhost:53858 /api/contacts,
    xhrFields: {
        withCredentials: true
    }
```

To allow credentials in cross-origin requests, the SupportsCredentials property should be set to true on the [EnableCors] attribute as given in the following code:

```
[EnableCors(origins: "http://chapter09client.com", headers: "*",
methods: "*", SupportsCredentials = true)]
```

The HTTP response will also have the Access-Control-Allow-Credentials header, to indicate to the browser that the server is fine to accept credentials in cross-origin requests. Using Cookie or Authorization header, Web API authenticates the request. Once authenticated, the browser will keep passing the authentication information on all subsequent requests to the server.

> Note that we cannot set the "*" wildcard value to the origins parameter and enable in order to support credentials at the same time.

If the response does not have the Access-Control-Allow-Credentials header, the AJAX call method will not receive the response as the browser doesn't expose it, this will cause the AJAX request to fail.

Enabling CORS at various scope

CORS can be enabled at various levels. We can set CORS at action level, controller level, or global level. Let's see how to set CORS at various scope.

Enable at action level

To enable CORS to a specific action, we need to decorate the action method with the [EnableCors] attribute as given in the following code snippet:

```
public class ContactsController : ApiController
{
    [EnableCors(origins: "http://localhost:53870", headers: "*",
methods: "*")]
    public HttpResponseMessage GetContacts() { ... }

    public HttpResponseMessage GetContact(int id) { ... }
    public HttpResponseMessage PostContact() { ... }
    public HttpResponseMessage PutContact(int id) { ... }
}
```

As you can see, CORS is only applicable for the GetContacts() action method.

Enable at controller level

We can also enable CORS at a specific controller. We just need to decorate the controller with the [EnableCors] attribute as follows:

```
[EnableCors(origins: "http://localhost:53870", headers: "*", methods:
"*")]
public class ContactsController : ApiController
{
    public HttpResponseMessage GetContacts() { ... }
    public HttpResponseMessage GetContact(int id) { ... }
    public HttpResponseMessage PostContact() { ... }
    public HttpResponseMessage PutContact(int id) { ... }
}
```

As you can see, CORS is applicable for any action in this controller. However, sometimes, you may want to disable CORS for one particular action. Let's say, we want to disable CORS for the PutContact() action method. This can be very easily achieved by decorating the PutContact() action using the [DisableCors] attribute as given in the following:

```
[EnableCors(origins: "http://chapter09client.com", headers: "*",
methods: "*")]
public class ContactsController : ApiController
{
    public HttpResponseMessage GetContacts() { ... }
    public HttpResponseMessage GetContact(int id) { ... }
    public HttpResponseMessage PostContact() { ... }

    [DisableCors]
    public HttpResponseMessage PutContact(int id) { ... }
}
```

If CORS is enabled at controller level and you would like to disable CORS for a specific method in the controller, then we can decorate such methods with the DisableCors attribute as given in the preceding code snippet.

Enable CORS globally

Sometimes, we may need to enable CORS to all controllers and actions in the Web API. In other words, we may need to enable CORS to the whole Web API.

This can be achieved by enabling CORS globally. We need to pass an instance of EnableCorsAttribute to the EnableCors method in HTTP configuration in the WebApiConfig file as given in the following:

```
public static class WebApiConfig
{
    public static void Register(HttpConfiguration config)
    {
        var cors = new EnableCorsAttribute("http://localhost:53870",
"*", "*");
        config.EnableCors(cors);
        // ...
    }
}
```

This global configuration can be overridden at controller or action level. The order of precedence will be action, controller, and global.

Summary

Woohoo! You just learned how to enable cross-origin request sharing (CORS) in our Web API.

You learned about what CORS is and how it works.

Then you learned some configuration stuff in setting up allowed origins, HTTP methods, request headers, and response headers.

Finally, you learned about passing credentials in cross-origin requests and enabling CORS at different scope in Web API.

Hurray! That's it, folks! Now, we know how to secure our Web API by adopting apt security solutions from various techniques available in the market.

Index

Symbol

[Authorize] attribute
  action level authorization filter 18
  controller level authorization filter 18
  global authorization filter 18
  using 17

A

access token
  obtaining 52-54
anti-forgery tokens
  AJAX used 111-113
  HTML Form used 110
  Razor View used 110
  working 111
ASP.NET Identity 2.1
  about 31
  setting up 30-35
ASP.NET Identity NuGet packages
  installing 30
ASP.NET MVC Application
  creating 86-88
ASP.NET Web API
  about 1
  Cross-Origin Resource Sharing (CORS),
      enabling 115
  security architecture 2
authenticated request
  sending 54, 55
authentication
  about 14, 15, 107
  implementing, in HTTP message
      handlers 15

authentication filter
  action-level 65
  combining, host-level authentication
      used 69, 70
  controller-level 66
  global-level 66
  setting 65
  used, for basic authentication 61-65
authorization
  about 14, 15
  inside controller action 19

B

basic authentication
  and Windows authentication,
      differentiating 81
  authentication filter used 61-65
  Internet Information Services (IIS)
      used 57, 58
  with custom membership 59, 60
browser client
  principal, setting up 17
  setting up 3
  Web API, consuming with JavaScript and
      jQuery 10, 11
  Web API lookup service, implementing 3, 4

C

client certificates
  IIS, configuring 25
  SSL Client Certificate, creating 24
  using, in Web API 23
  verifying, in Web API 25

S

Secure Sockets Layer (SSL)
about 21
enforcing, in Web API controller 21-23
SSL Client Certificate
creating 24

T

Transport Level Security (TLS) 21
Twitter authentication
implementing 95-98

U

unauthorized request
sending 49-51

W

Web API
adding, to OWIN 41-47
application, running 14
authentication filter, implementing 66-68
Authorization Filters 2
client certificates, using 23
client certificates, verifying 25
consuming, with JavaScript and
  jQuery 10, 11
contact list, obtaining 13
contact, obtaining by ID 13
controllers, defining 35-37
Forms authentication, implementing 72-77
Message Handler 2
methods, defining 35-37
Web API lookup service
controller, adding 6-9
implementing 3, 4
model, adding 4, 5
Windows authentication
and basic authentication, differentiating 81
configuring 77-80
enabling, in Katana 81-83

Thank you for buying
ASP.NET Web API Security Essentials

About Packt Publishing

Packt, pronounced 'packed', published its first book, *Mastering phpMyAdmin for Effective MySQL Management*, in April 2004, and subsequently continued to specialize in publishing highly focused books on specific technologies and solutions.

Our books and publications share the experiences of your fellow IT professionals in adapting and customizing today's systems, applications, and frameworks. Our solution-based books give you the knowledge and power to customize the software and technologies you're using to get the job done. Packt books are more specific and less general than the IT books you have seen in the past. Our unique business model allows us to bring you more focused information, giving you more of what you need to know, and less of what you don't.

Packt is a modern yet unique publishing company that focuses on producing quality, cutting-edge books for communities of developers, administrators, and newbies alike. For more information, please visit our website at www.packtpub.com.

About Packt Open Source

In 2010, Packt launched two new brands, Packt Open Source and Packt Enterprise, in order to continue its focus on specialization. This book is part of the Packt Open Source brand, home to books published on software built around open source licenses, and offering information to anybody from advanced developers to budding web designers. The Open Source brand also runs Packt's Open Source Royalty Scheme, by which Packt gives a royalty to each open source project about whose software a book is sold.

Writing for Packt

We welcome all inquiries from people who are interested in authoring. Book proposals should be sent to author@packtpub.com. If your book idea is still at an early stage and you would like to discuss it first before writing a formal book proposal, then please contact us; one of our commissioning editors will get in touch with you.

We're not just looking for published authors; if you have strong technical skills but no writing experience, our experienced editors can help you develop a writing career, or simply get some additional reward for your expertise.

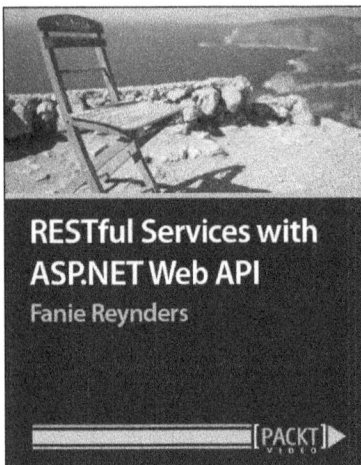

RESTful Services with ASP.NET Web API [Video]

ISBN: 978-1-78328-575-4   Duration: 02:04 hrs

Get hands-on experience of building RESTful services for the modern Web using ASP.NET Web API

1. Apply your current ASP.NET knowledge to make your Web APIs more secure and comply to the global standard in order to make your service RESTful.

2. Explore the possibilities of extending your Web APIs by making use of message handlers, filters, and media formatters.

3. Comprehensive examples to help you build an end-to-end working solution for a real-use case.

ASP.NET Web API: Build RESTful web applications and services on the .NET framework

ISBN: 978-1-84968-974-8   Paperback: 224 pages

Master ASP.NET Web API using .NET Framework 4.5 and Visual Studio 2013

1. Clear and concise guide to the ASP.NET Web API with plentiful code examples.

2. Learn about the advanced concepts of the WCF-windows communication foundation.

3. Explore ways to consume Web API services using ASP.NET, ASP.NET MVC, WPF, and Silverlight clients.

Please check **www.PacktPub.com** for information on our titles

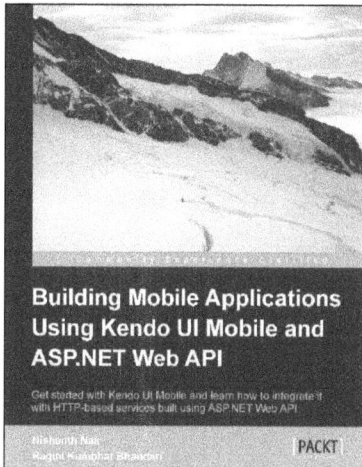

Building Mobile Applications Using Kendo UI Mobile and ASP.NET Web API

ISBN: 978-1-78216-092-2   Paperback: 256 pages

Get started with Kendo UI Mobile and learn how to integrate it with HTTP-based services built using ASP.NET Web API

1. Learn the basics of developing mobile applications using HTML5 and create an end-to-end mobile application from scratch.

2. Discover all about Kendo UI Mobile, ASP .NET Web API, and how to integrate them.

3. Understand how to organize your JavaScript code to achieve extensibility and maintainability.

ASP.NET MVC 4 Mobile App Development

ISBN: 978-1-84968-736-2   Paperback: 356 pages

Create next-generation applications for smart phones, tablets, and mobile devices using the ASP.NET MVC development framework

1. Learn and utilize the latest Microsoft tools and technologies to develop mobile web apps with a native feel.

2. Create web applications for the traditional and mobile web.

3. Discover techniques used to overcome the pitfalls of developing Internet-ready apps.

Please check **www.PacktPub.com** for information on our titles

www.ingramcontent.com/pod-product-compliance
Lightning Source LLC
Chambersburg PA
CBHW081540220326
41598CB00036B/6504